SUPER TOYS

DIY Projects to Support Sensory Processing

By
Kristin Cockrell, MOT, OTR/L
Melissa Haworth

Photography
Karin Higgins Sturgis

Roxy in the Heavy Hero weighted shirt.

This book is dedicated to our families:

Rob
Paige
Charlie

Jake
Kyson
Declan
McKenna

We love you.

Dear Reader:

Thank you for buying this book! Creating it has been an exciting journey. We first talked about the need for this book, and even wrote a rough draft, the weekend we were hanging out in San Diego for our 20-year high school reunion. Yes, we went to high school together. Since then, some of the projects have changed but our goal hasn't: to give parents and professionals a way to make the toys and tools most often recommended by therapists for children with sensory challenges. Oh, and the projects aren't just for children diagnosed with Sensory Processing Disorder--they are lots of fun for all kids (just ask our children).

Kristin works as an occupational therapist. She came up with the list of projects based on what she most frequently recommends to parents who bring their kids to her practice. Melissa worked with Kristin to develop the ideas into specific patterns and create the step-by-step instructions you'll find inside. We tried hard to include variations on each project to make them simpler, cheaper, or more personal.

Of course, even though Kristin is a licensed therapist and provides an overview of the sensory systems, this book is not a substitute for diagnosis, nor does it replace individual therapy provided by a professional. The projects are meant to support your child's current therapy and enhance their ability to integrate the sensory systems.

We hope you have a wonderful time creating these projects and that your children love them! Please, share what you've made using the hashtag #DIYSuperToys on social media. Also be sure to visit our website DIYSuperToys.com where we have links to video content and where we will post any corrections or updates.

We can't wait to see what you make!
Kristin and Melissa
October 2015

Table of Contents

LET'S GET STARTED

PROPRIOCEPTION

VESTIBULAR

TACTILE

Super Simple Projects

OTHER SENSES (AUDITORY, VISUAL, ORAL, OLFACTORY)

Super Simple Projects

MORE INFORMATION

ABOUT SENSORY PROCESSING

Sensory processing is a term that refers to how we take in and react to the different types of information coming into our body through our senses: sight, hearing, taste, smell, touch, pain and temperature, pressure, and even the force of gravity on our bodies and our body's position in space.

Interconnected systems

The many sensory systems are complex and interconnected; it is not as simple as the five senses you learned about in school. How we respond to sensory input can be measured on a continuum from hyporesponsive (under-responsive) to hyperresponsive (over-responsive). Most people fall somewhere in the middle of the continuum for all sensory input. However, it is very common for people to have different response levels for different sensory systems. For example, someone might be hyperresponsive to auditory input and hyporesponsive to proprioceptive input--that is, input about the body's movement and position in space.

Gathering environmental information

When our body accurately interprets sensory input, we can use it to gather information necessary to safely navigate our environment. Imagine you are cleaning splattered sauce off your stove. You sense heat and pain in your fingertips; you hear a sizzle; perhaps you smell singed cotton. What do you do? You move your hand quickly! You tell yourself: I'd better turn off that burner right now! But what if your senses failed to signal you to turn off the stove?

Supporting the sensory systems

Activities and tools that provide the right amount of input to the targeted sensory system can help children feel more calm, relaxed and happy, thereby reducing over-responsiveness and negative behaviors. This is often referred to as "organizing" input. Activities that enhance the sensory input coming into the body, increasing awareness and responsiveness, are referred to as "alerting" input.

Sensory processing disorder

When there is a breakdown between how the information is coming in, or how it is interpreted, behaviors that are inappropriate for the situation often arise. These behaviors might take the form of disruptions in the classroom, difficulty falling asleep at night, hanging on mom's leg during a party, refusal to eat certain foods, inattentiveness, or avoiding activities other children undertake with gusto, such as climbing on a jungle gym. Individuals whose day to day life functions are significantly impaired because of challenges in processing sensory input may be diagnosed as having a Sensory Processing Disorder (SPD). We recommend working with your healthcare provider to understand your child's specific needs. See the chapter introductions and Resources section for books and websites that provide a more in depth explanation of SPD.

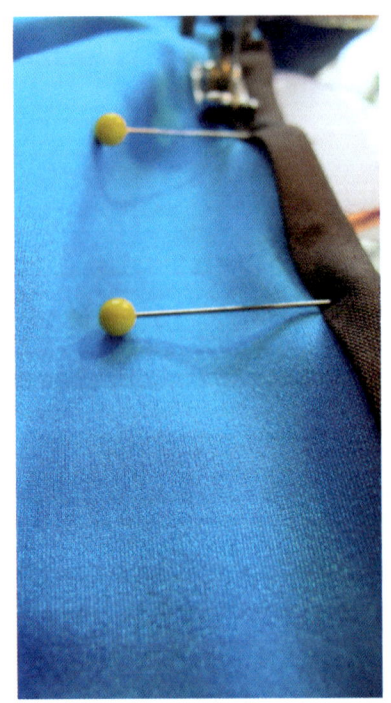

Tools that can help

In recent years, more parents, teachers, and professionals have discovered that some children's challenging behaviors may be attributed to deficits in sensory processing. This increased awareness has led to a rise in the availability of commercial products to support sensory processing. However, many of those resources can be quite expensive and aren't always exactly right for each child's individual needs. This book provides detailed instructions to make your own tools.

Some toys in this book are designed to be used away from home. We encourage you to talk with your child's teachers and with other professionals about how these sensory toys and tools can be used in the classroom or other non-home environment.

THE PROJECTS

The projects in Super Toys are divided into four chapters based on major sensory systems: Proprioceptive, Vestibular, Tactile, and the "Other" senses, which includes Visual, Oral, Olfactory and Auditory. The 16 more elaborate projects in the book cover all the major sensory systems and are complemented by 27 "Super Simple" projects that are quick to create and often use common household items. Just because they're easy to make doesn't mean the super simple projects aren't great tools for your children.

Because there is so much overlap between different sensory systems, some projects in the book support more than one system. Therefore each project is labeled in the top right corner with icon(s) for relevant sensory system(s). And, of course, these toys are meant to support all children's sensory processing, regardless of whether a child has a specific diagnosis.

The joy of making rather than buying is that you can create a toy tailored to your child's needs and tastes while infusing the projects with your love and caring.

As you explore these projects, keep in mind that you are trying to find that "just right" fit for your child.   These projects are designed to be a jumping off point for your own creativity. We hope you will use the instructions as a guide to create something as unique as your child.

Please be safe. Be sure to examine each toy regularly for wear and supervise children to ensure the projects are being used in a safe manner.

SEWING INFORMATION

The projects that involve sewing are written for machine sewing. If you can operate your sewing machine and sew a reasonably straight seam you are all set. You will also need the sewing supplies listed on the following page. All seam allowances are ¼ inch unless otherwise noted. And you won't find any pattern pieces to trace in this book. Instead we provide measurements you can use to cut basic shapes while allowing maximum flexibility to adjust the project size to meet your needs.

If you need help getting started with your machine, YouTube is a great resource for videos on threading and winding bobbins for many machine models. Instructables.com is another website with a wealth of useful tutorials. And, of course, there are numerous sewing books, knowledgeable friends and family, and local sewing stores. We have posted instructional videos on YouTube to support several of the projects. For links, go to diysupertoys.com.

SEWING SUPPLIES

You will need to purchase or borrow the following supplies to successfully complete the sewing projects:

Basic sewing supplies: scissors, pins, thread, iron, tape measure, straight edge ruler

- A basic sewing machine for straight and zigzag stitches
- Sewing machine needles
- All purpose thread
- Fabric scissors
- Straight pins
- Disappearing fabric pen or chalk marking pencil
- Straight edge, such as a yardstick
- Tape measure
- Iron

For many projects it is very nice to have a rotary cutter, 6 x 24 inch clear plastic ruler and self healing mat but these tools are not necessary for success. If you want to invest, all of these items are commonly used for quilting and available at any large fabric store. Many of the photos show a rotary cutter but instead of a rotary cutter, you can mark a straight line with your chalk pencil and use scissors to cut.

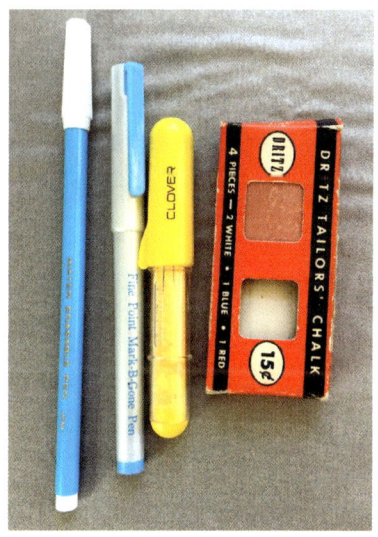

Various tools for marking fabric. We primarily used the yellow Clover brand chalk wheel

POLY PELLETS AND OTHER WEIGHTS

Poly pellets are small plastic beads used for weighting a variety of children's toys. We ordered the white, non-smooth pellets shown in this book from http://qualityplasticpellets.com/ but a quick internet search will show several vendors. Watch out—shipping can be very expensive, so be sure to comparison shop with shipping costs included.

The advantage of poly pellets is that they are machine washable and won't deteriorate over time. But they are expensive. Rice or dry beans may be substituted in some projects as long as the weights are removable or the project won't get wet. Or, if it may get wet, encase the beans/rice in plastic bags before covering with fabric. If you want to recycle, consider using a plastic bread bag rather than a grocery bag. The plastic of many disposable grocery bags makes a sound that may be distressing; bread bags or newspaper bags are quieter. In some cases, sand may also be used as a weight, though it is less flexible and very heavy.

Feel free to substitute different substances in your projects to achieve different weights and functionality.

STRETCHY FABRIC

Purchasing Lycra, spandex or other knit, stretchy fabrics can be confusing. Some retailers and manufacturers call fabric that stretches in both directions (along the length and width) "four way" stretch but others call it "two way" stretch. If at all possible, go to a local fabric store and stretch the fabric for yourself--you need a fabric that stretches in both directions.

For projects that call for Lycra it need not be brand name. Look for swim or dancewear fabric which is a heavy duty spandex blend with plenty of stretch in both directions. It typically costs about $16 per yard. Avoid lightweight, inexpensive polyester knits made for garment sewing--they often only stretch in one direction and are too flimsy for these projects.

Finding the right cotton or polyester knits for projects like the Squeezy Sheets can be tricky. You'll want something similar to a jersey t-shirt knit but a bit heavier and with much more stretch. When pulled, the fabric should stretch to almost double its original length and quickly pop back to its original size.The knit fabric found in the nursery section of your local fabric store is not stretchy enough. You might have better luck at a remnant store.

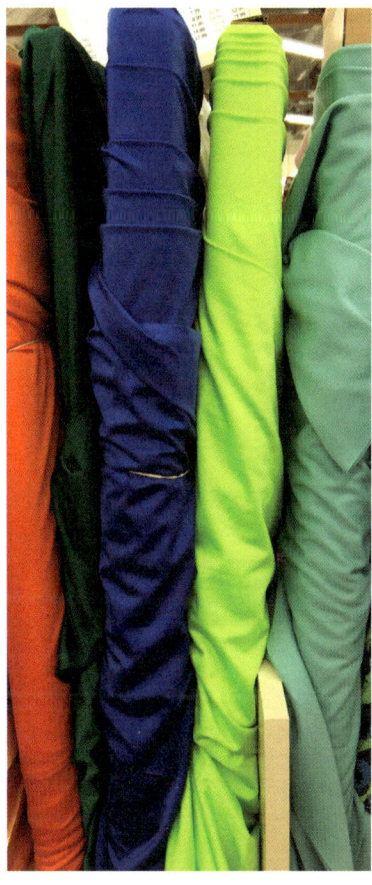

ABOUT NEEDLES

There are machine sewing needles made just for sewing knits and stretchy fabric. Ball point needles are good for jersey fabric and stretch needles are good for Lycra. Depending on your machine you may be able to use them interchangeably.

We recommend purchasing a pack of specialized needles for the knit and stretchy fabric-based projects in this book.

Carlos reading under a Heavy Blanket

Seth is a spontaneous, fun-loving seven-year-old boy. As an infant, the only thing that calmed him was to be tightly swaddled or worn in a wrap-style carrier. As soon as he could move, he would choose to position himself in small, cramped spaces wherever he could find them. Now that he is in school, Seth often stands too close to the other kids in line. A few of his classmates have complained that he also sits too close to them on the rug. Seth even invented a game at home where he climbs between his mom and the back of the sofa and asks her to lean against him (he calls the game Squishes). Seth's favorite activities are wrestling his older brother, diving for saves as goalkeeper of his soccer team, and climbing trees in the backyard.

Over time, his parents have worked with seth's teachers and found that movement breaks of running and jumping help decrease his "squishing" and other distracting movements, such as tilting his chair backwards until falling out. Walking home from school with a heavy backpack helps prepare him for homework. Finding the right outlets helps him feel calmer and makes him more successful overall.

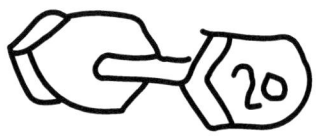

Proprioception is the sensory system that identifies body position and movement in space using information provided by pressure sensors in our skin, muscles, and joints. This information helps the body identify how hard to push, which body part to move and where, and provides information to the rest of the body for balance and movement against gravity. Using the proprioceptive system, the body unconsciously makes postural adjustments, varies the amount of force applied when completing a task, and senses where it is in space.

Heavy work and deep pressure are two ways to target the proprioceptive system. Heavy work can be obtained by engaging in resistive activities that push and pull our joints, stretch our muscles, and provide movement against gravity. Deep pressure is a widely used relaxation technique. We wrap our arms around our children when they are upset or injured, we give strong hugs to friends who are upset or grieving, and a massage can help us wind down at the end of a long day. Deep pressure targets receptors in the body (proprioceptors) that calm the nervous system so that an individual can more accurately interpret the various tactile, auditory, and visual inputs coming into their body.

CHARACTERISTICS TYPICAL OF A CHILD WITH PROPRIOCEPTIVE SENSITIVITY

awkward or uncoordinated movement

avoids movement

difficulty with stairs

poor balance

no sense of personal space

bumps and crashes purposefully

frequently breaks toys

presses too light or too hard when writing

enjoys wrestling with others

plays too rough with people and/or animals

seeks bear hugs or squishes

seeks or avoids crunchy or chewy foods

overstuffs mouth

difficulty with kicking or throwing at a target

In the proprioception chapter

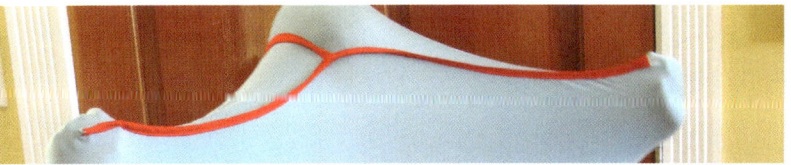

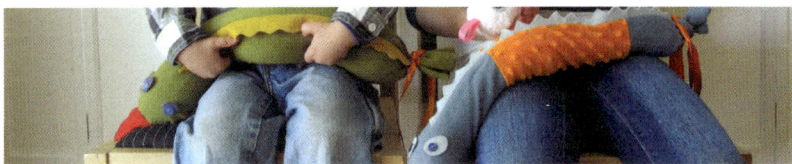
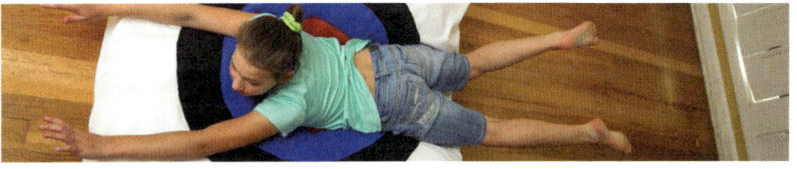

Paige inside the Stretchy Cocoon

Stretchy Cocoon

Much like the Heavy Blanket (page 38) the Stretchy Cocoon provides gentle resistance and calming pressure. It is great for kids who crave hugs, squishes, and small spaces. The cocoon also allows children to exert themselves against the resistance of the stretchy fabric. Children can stand and push their arms outward or lie down and move their entire body against the stretchy fabric. For children who seek proprioceptive or deep pressure input, inside this cocoon is where they'll want to be!

Sewing Lycra on a household sewing machine is very difficult. Standard sewing machine stitches, even a zig zag, don't stretch as much as the fabric, so the seams tear out. The solution for this project is to use bias tape to make sure the seams don't stretch at all, and thus don't break.

MATERIALS

Four-way stretch spandex or Lycra fabric approximately 54 inches wide. Length depends on the size of the child, see below.

1 package of double fold bias tape (3 yards)

Machine sewing supplies

Look for swimsuit or dancewear fabric at the store and tug on it to ensure it has plenty of stretch in all directions. Also, put the fabric up to your face and ensure you can see and breathe through the fabric. You don't want anything so heavy or dark it might be frightening for your child.

The cocoon should be sized for the user. But because the fabric stretches the size does not have to be precise. Measure the height of your child to her shoulder. Purchase approximately this length of Lycra rounded up to the nearest partial yard increment. My child is 45 inches from floor to shoulder so I purchased 1 1/3 yards (48 inches) of fabric.

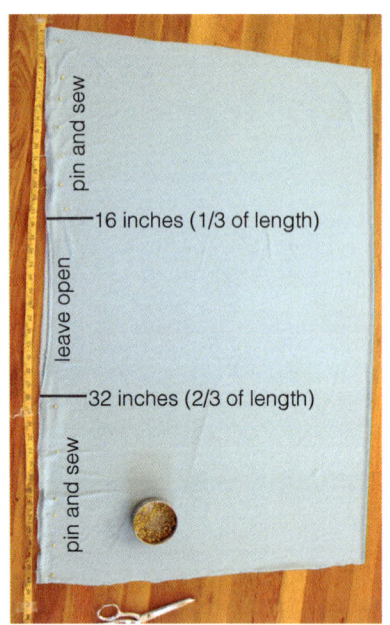

The top and bottom thirds of the selvage edge are pinned.

The bias tape is sewn over the seam--note that the seam allowance is inside but is fully encased in the bias tape. At the opening in the middle, shown here, the raw edge of the bias tape is tucked underneath.

1. Fold your fabric in half from selvage to selvage. The rectangle should be 27 inches wide for 54 inch fabric. Note that most Lycra doesn't have a "good" side but if you have printed Lycra, fold good sides together. Pin along the selvage edge.

2. Measure along the selvage, dividing the length into thirds. For example, if the fabric is be 48 inches long you will make a mark at 16 inches and 32 inches.

3. Sew with a scant ¼ inch seam allowance from the top to the first mark. Stop and sew again from the second mark to the bottom. The middle 1/3 of your seam along the selvage edge should be left open.

4. Turn the fabric inside out so the seam allowance is now inside. Starting at one end, pin bias tape over the selvage edge seam enclosing the seam allowance inside the cocoon. The narrower side of the bias tape should face up to ensure you catch the back of the bias tape as you sew. At the open gap in the middle, fold the edge of the bias tape in to hide the raw edge. Sew the bias tape in place.

5. Turn the cocoon inside out again so the bias tape is now inside. Spread out the cocoon with the seam facing up and centered on the Lycra. Pin the top and bottom of the cocoon and stitch all the the way across the top and bottom edges with a scant ¼ inch seam. You will sew over the bias tape in the center of each seam.

As before, turn inside out and cover the seam with stitched on bias tape, folding in the raw ends of the bias tape at each end of the cocoon.

6. That's it! The selvage edge at the opening can be left unfinished--it will not unravel and will have plenty of stretch, allowing the child to squeeze into the cocoon and stretch to their heart's delight. The cocoon can be used with the bias tape facing out as a design element or facing in to be hidden.

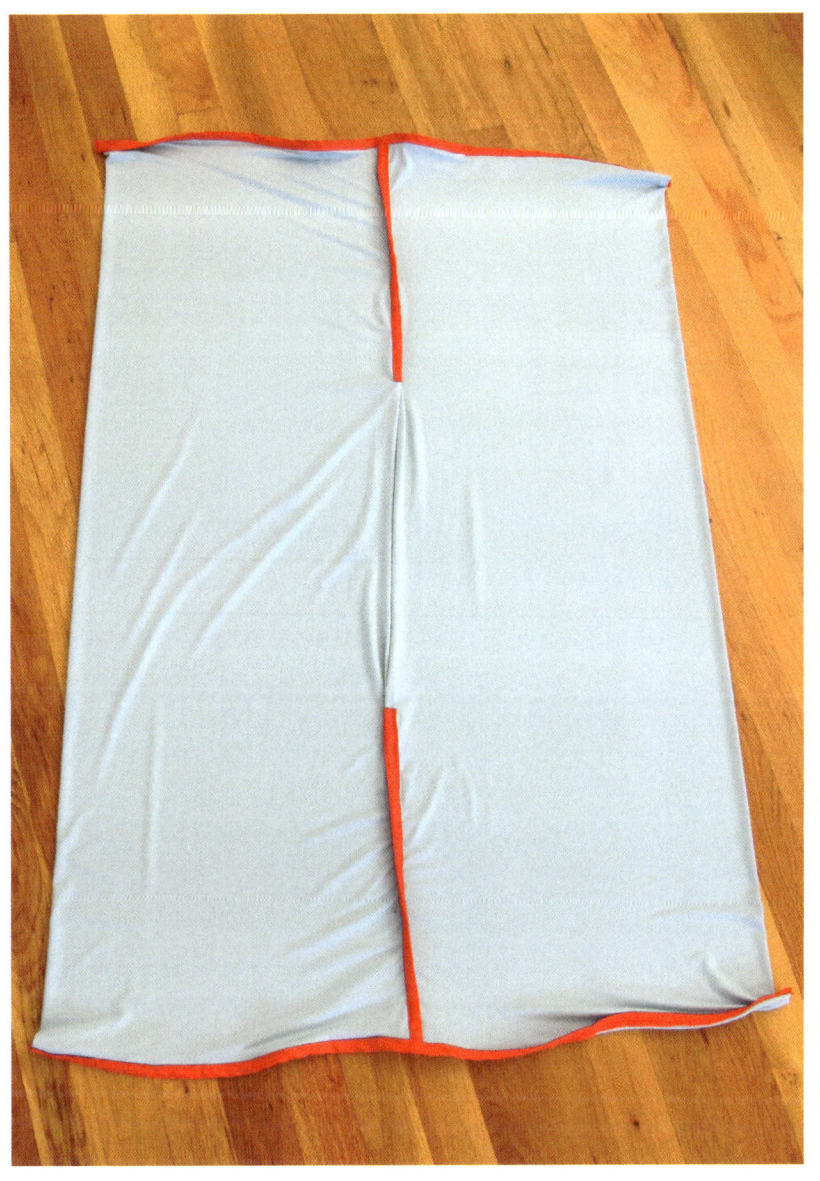

The completed cocoon showing the layout of the seams.

The bias tape is pinned to sew over the seam along the top and bottom thirds of the selvage edge. (step 4)

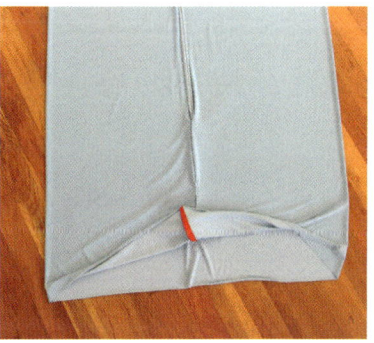

Ready to pin and sew the top and bottom of the cocoon. Note the first seam is inside.

The top and bottom edge are pinned. Once sewn they will be turned inside out and covered with bias tape.

23

Charlie playing in the Heavy Hero weighted shirt and cuffs

Heavy Hero

Occupational therapists often recommend weighted garments, such as vests, to provide proprioceptive input through the shoulders and trunk. Weighted vests can be quite expensive and may not always be the most fashionable. This project is a fun alternative to a vest style weighted garment. The Heavy Hero is a shirt that functions just like a weighted vest, is customizable, and is easy to make. Even more, it's a fun super hero costume! You can even make weighted cuffs for added proprioceptive input at the wrists.

As written, this project is sized for younger children, ages four to seven. However, the approach to creating a weighted shirt can be adapted for people of all sizes. The weighted inserts can be added or removed to adjust the weight for the child and the situation.

The shirt should be worn when the child is being supervised. Because of the weight the child will need assistance putting on and removing the shirt.

MATERIALS

Two identical t-shirts sized to fit your child

½ yard rip stop nylon in a coordinating color

½ yard Lycra fabric

Sand

6" sew on Velcro, ¾ inch wide

Machine sewing supplies

The shirts should ideally be identical but you can use shirts that have the same length and width. A shirt made of high quality knit with a sturdy neckline will work best for this project. A raglan style t-shirt (like the Superman shirt in the images) stretches more than a traditional t-shirt at the neckline so is not the best choice.

Weighted tubes slide into the shirt so weight is easily adjusted and tubes can be removed for washing.

Put one shirt inside the other so wrong sides are together.

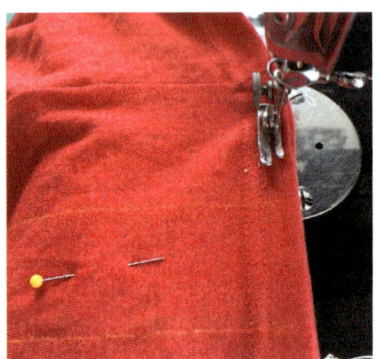

Sew around bottom hems twice. Note pins in channels.

Mark vertical channels with a chalk pencil.

1. Put the shirts together. Turn one shirt inside out and put it inside the other shirt. The wrong sides of the shirts should be facing each other. Smooth the shirts and ensure they are lined up at the side seams. Using a coordinating thread, sew the shirts together around the bottom hem, then make a second line of stitching for added security. This seam holds the weights in place.

2. Mark the shirts. Find the center front of the shirt and use a chalk pencil to draw a vertical line from the bottom hem to the neckline. Measure over 1.5 inches and draw another vertical line. Repeat on both sides of the center line until there are six columns marked on the shirt front. Repeat this pattern on the shirt back. Measure from the bottom hem to the neckline. This will be about 15 inches on a 5T shirt. Draw a horizontal line at this height across the front and the back. This will be the height of the channels and can be adjusted depending on the size of shirt you use. The marks should not be on the collar or sleeve areas.

3. Sew columns for the weights. Pin the shirt layers inside the marked columns. Using a coordinating thread, sew along the marked vertical lines from the bottom hem to the mark approximately 15 inches from the bottom. This will create channels between the shirts. Do not sew across the tops of the channels or around the neckline of the shirts.

4. Decide on the size of the weighted tubes. The overall weight of the vest will depend how large you make the weighted tubes that will slip into the channels on the shirt made in the previous step. If the nylon is cut 3.25 inches wide and filled with playground sand, a 15-inch long tube weighs about 7 ounces. A 3 inch wide tube weighs about 6 ounces. Up to 12 weighted tubes can be used in the vest. The overall weight of the vest should be 5-10% of the child's body weight so the tubes should be sized and filled accordingly. The weight can also be adjusted by using more or fewer filled tubes in the shirt.

5. Sew the tubes. Cut the ripstop nylon into 12 strips of the width determined in the previous step. The strips should be 18 inches tall if you purchased ½ yard of nylon. Fold each rectangle in half lengthwise and sew down one long side and across one narrow end using a short stitch length and locking stitches at the end. Stitch this seam again within the seam allowance so you have two parallel stitching lines quite close together. Use a pencil to turn the tubes right side out.

6. Fill the tubes. Fill the tubes to about 15 inches high with sand. A simple cone of paper makes an easy funnel. Confirm the height of the sand compared to the height of the shirt channels. Trim the top of the tube if needed, leaving at least one inch of fabric above the sand. Fold over the top edge twice and stitch to secure.

Make the cape.

1. Cut a rectangle of Lycra a bit larger than the back of the shirt. For a 5T t-shirt the rectangle would be 15 x 18 inches.

2. Sew Velcro. Attach 1.5 inches of the soft side of the Velcro to the back of the shoulder of the outside shirt. Make sure you don't sew the two shirts together at this step. Sew the hook side of the Velcro to the top two corners of the cape across a 15-inch edge on the wrong side of the Lycra.

Make the wrist weights.

The size of the wrist weights can be adjusted to the size of the child but there is a lot of stretch. The dimensions below are based on a 5-inch wrist circumference.

1. Cut two rectangles of Lycra 10 x 5.5 inches. Fold the rectangle in half, good side out, and at one end, position a 1.5 inch piece of Velcro parallel to the length of the cuff and nearly centered on the folded Lycra. The Velcro should be a bit more toward the folded side to account for the seam allowance. Unfold the fabric, pin the Velcro and sew it in place.

The channels are sewn. Note that the top of each channel is open.

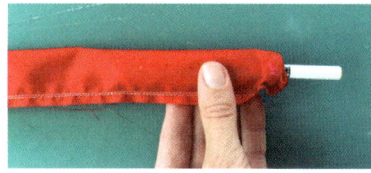

Turn the nylon tubes inside out using a pen. Notice the double rows of stitching.

A simple cone of rolled paper makes an easy funnel to fill the tubes with sand.

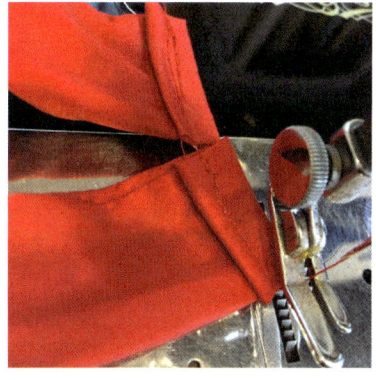

Sew the tubes closed. You may need to cut off excess fabric to achieve the right length.

First sew the velcro to the fabric before making the wrist weight.

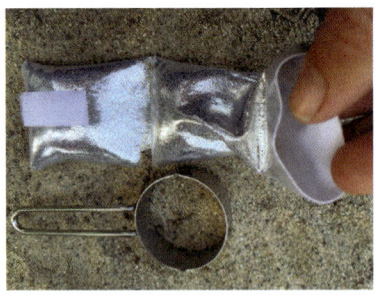

Fill partially with sand and stitch to secure before adding more sand.

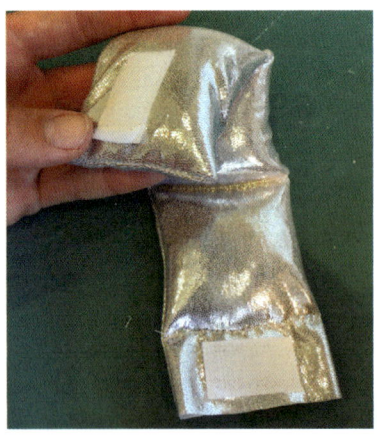

The completed wrist weight. Note the velcro placement.

2. Fold the Lycra in half with good sides together (the Velcro will now be inside) and stitch across the Velcro end and up the long side opposite the fold, using a very short stitch length. Stitch a second seam as you did for the weighted tubes--this prevents the sand from leaking. Turn the tube right side out.

3. Add sand. Pour in approximately ¼ cup or enough to lightly fill about ¼ of the cuff length. Stitch across the cuff above the sand. Add more sand and stitch again. Add a third bit of sand and stitch to secure, leaving a one to two inch tab at the open end. Sew the other side of the Velcro onto this tab. Be sure to wrap the cuff around your wrist to ensure you stitch it to the right side--the Velcro on the tab should be on the opposite side of the cuff from the Velcro sewed in Step 2. Test the size on your child's wrist and repeat to make a second cuff adjusting as needed.

CHEAPER

Use recycled t-shirts for the main project.

Use t-shirt or jersey knit rather than Lycra for the cape and wrist weights. Make sure to use a high quality knit so the sand can't leak through.

EASIER

Skip the cape and/or wristbands.

FANCIER

Embellish the cape with felt symbols.

Use a patterned shirt, as shown in some of the above photos, or decorate or tie dye a plain shirt before beginning the directions.

HARDWARE PENCIL WEIGHT

Glue bolts and washers to the top of the pencil just below the eraser. Or use rubber washers that fit the pencil on either end of the washers. The added weight provides additional proprioceptive input for children who have difficulty with pencil grasp and writing tasks.

HAIR TIE PENCIL HOLDER

This pencil holder helps those who have a hard time maintaining an efficient pencil grasp or have difficulty with joint positioning and motor planning. Use a narrow, elastic headband knotted near one end or two elastic hair ties knotted together. Slip the larger loop over the wrist and place the pencil in the smaller loop. The elastic will pull the eraser side of the pencil back toward the shoulder to promote a mature pencil grasp.

Heather reading with a Weighty Worm.

Weighty Worm

These little "worms" are a great, portable tool. When used as a lap buddy resting on the child's legs, it provides deep pressure input, which has a calming and organizing effect on the body, reducing the need to move and fidget. When carried around or transported in a backpack, the weight of the Weighty Worm provides additional proprioceptive input to the child, which will help their body to navigate their environment. The various textures provide fun fidget opportunities for any child whose hands like to explore their (or their neighbor's) belongings when sitting quietly in the classroom, church, or car. These are quick and fun to make and can easily be personalized for any child.

MATERIALS

One adult tube sock

2-3 pounds of poly pellets

Scrap of knit fabric, at least 10 x 30 inches

Sturdy rubber band

Embellishment materials such as buttons, wool felt, textured fabrics or fleece, ribbons

Machine sewing supplies

A ball point needle for sewing knit fabrics

Hand sewing needle

Poly pellets are great because they can get wet, but the worm can also be filled with rice or beans. The advantage of rice is that the inside sock (and possibly the entire worm, depending on materials chosen) can be microwaved for soothing warmth.

Filling the sock with poly pellets. A small embroidery hoop is holding the sock open.

Sewing the filled sock closed.

Felt, fleece, ribbon and buttons for embellishments.

1. Fill the sock. Pour the poly pellets or other filling material into the sock until it is full, but not stuffed. You want the sock to be able to bend. Stitch the top of sock closed on the sewing machine. Measure the length and average circumference of your filled sock. Don't worry about a bulbous toe or heel--it all works out.

2. Cut fabric for the worm body. Cut a rectangle of the knit fabric that is 1 inch wider than the sock circumference and 5 inches longer than the filled sock length. For example, if your sock is 20 inches long and 7 inches around, cut your fabric to 8 x 25 inches.

If desired, cut a ridged spine from felt approximately 1-1.5 inches tall and tapered at the ends. The spine should be 6-8 inches shorter than the piece of fabric cut for the body.

3. Sew worm body. Fold the body fabric in half lengthwise with good sides together. If you are inserting a spine piece, place it between the pieces of body fabric with the flat edge lined up with the edge of the body fabric. Position the spine one inch down from one end. Pin and sew along the long edge using a quarter inch seam. Leave both ends open.

4. Round out the worm's head and add a tongue. Place the worm body on the table, still inside out and with the back seam facing up and centered. Draw a curved line as shown in the photo to round off the end. If you inserted a spine, the head should be at the end where the spine is only one inch from the opening.

Cut a piece of fleece or ribbon to create a tongue and place it between the layers of the head. The tip of the tongue should be inside the worm body and the raw edge should be aligned with the end of the worm. Fleece and felt do not unravel so you can leave an unfinished edge. For ribbon, fold the ribbon in half so the cut ends are sewn into the body. Pin the tongue in place and sew along your curved line. Then trim excess fabric to leave approximately a quarter inch seam allowance.

5. Add the weighted sock. Turn your worm body right side out and slide in the weighted sock. Depending how stretchy your worm fabric is, it can take a bit of effort to squeeze the sock in, but keep at it. On the tail end, you should have nearly five inches of fabric extending beyond the end of the sock. You can tie this fabric into a knot or secure it closed with a rubber band so it can easily be opened to remove the cover for cleaning.

6. Embellish the worm. To position eyes and other embellishments precisely you'll want to add these to your worm after it's stuffed. The trick is to sew on any extra pieces without sewing the worm body to the sock inside. If your worm is for an older child, buttons make great eyes and can be backed with an oval of felt. For younger children, felt eyes or safety eyes will eliminate the choking hazard. Ribbons may be added to the tail for added texture.

CHEAPER

An outgrown t-shirt would provide perfect knit fabric for the worm body. And, of course, use a sock whose mate is lost or holey.

Fill the worm with rice or beans rather than poly pellets. If you don't plan to microwave a rice filled sock, consider using a plastic newspaper bag or bread bag inside the sock to prevent the beans or rice from getting wet.

EASIER

Simply stuff a sock with poly pellets to create a soothing lap weight. You can decorate it with fabric markers or paint... or not.

FANCIER

This is perfect project to embellish to your heart's content --perhaps even in collaboration with its recipient.

The body can be a patchwork of different fabrics to incorporate different textures. For example, sew together strips of different fleece or knit to construct a rectangle of the necessary size. If your fabrics aren't very stretchy, add at least 1/2 inch to the width of the worm body. You can also incorporate highly textured fabrics such as the polyester dusting mitt fabric shown on the pink worm or other fabrics shown as part of the Texture Quilt on page 68.

Allow your child to decorate the worm with fabric pens or fabric paints. This can be done on the fabric before sewing or after the worm is assembled.

Place the spine fabric inside the folded body fabric.

The tongues are tucked inside and the body is pinned and ready to sew the curve of the nose.

The worm nose is sewn and trimmed.

The body fabric can be a patchwork of different textures.

Jacob landing on Target Crash Pillow

Target Crash Pillow

The Target Crash Pillow is perfect for children who jump on or into the furniture, enjoy being squished up in blankets and pillows, or seek out bump and crash activities. It's almost as good as having a foam pit in your house! The crash pillow has a removable, washable cover and the graphic target motif will look cool in a kid's play space or your living room. In addition to being a soft landing place for jumps and dives, it can also be useful beneath a swing or underneath a child playing in a Stretchy Cocoon (see page 20).

Finished size is about 44 by 49 inches and 12 inches thick.

MATERIALS

2.5 yards of heavyweight, washable white fabric 58-60 inches wide

1 yard black fleece

7/8 yard blue or turquoise fleece

½ yard red fleece

¼ yard yellow fleece

3 yards of any solid, woven fabric 45 inches wide (muslin is perfect).

A very large trash bag full of upholstery foam scraps

Permanent marker (such as Sharpie brand)

String that won't stretch

Machine sewing supplies

Look in the apparel fabrics section for fabrics labeled "bottomweights." These are often a sturdy, wrinkle resistant blend of polyester and cotton. They are perfect for this project.

This craft involves sewing multiple layers of thick fabric, so make sure your sewing machine and needle can accommodate this.

Cushion foam, rather than batting, is essential for safety. Purchasing new foam is very expensive, but some upholstery shops sell scraps at low prices or give them away, so don't be afraid to ask. You can also collect old couch cushions to cut up.

Mark the string at 4, 8, 12 nd 16 inches to make a "compass"

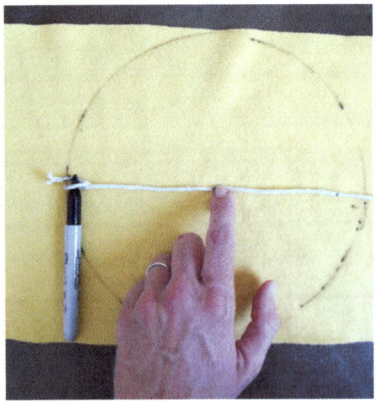

Hold the string and use the tied on pen to draw perfect circles.

Pin and then stitch the target to the pillow fabric. Note that the stitching is very close to the edge of the circle.

1. Make two large, white rectangles. Fold the white fabric in half to make a rectangle 58 inches (or your fabric width) by 45 inches. Cut in half along the fold. From one piece, cut 8 inches off one selvedge edge so the resulting rectangle is 45 x 50 inches. Set this piece aside. Fold the other piece in half again to make a rectangle 45 x 29 inches. Cut along the fold.

2. Hem one 45 inch long edge on each of the pieces that are 45 x 29 inches. Set the hemmed pieces aside.

3. Cut circles out of fleece fabrics. To mark perfect circles, tie your sturdy string to the permanent pen. Measure away from the pen and mark on the string at four, eight, 12 and 16 inches.

On the yellow fleece mark a light dot in the center of the width near one end. Hold the string at the 4" mark on the center dot and use the pen to draw a perfect circle. You may need to adjust your hold on the center of the string to allow it to rotate. Also be sure the pen is held perpendicular to the string. This can be a bit tricky but you have plenty of yellow fleece to practice with.

Mark the the other fabrics in the same manner using the different measurements on the string (red=eight inch, blue=12 inch, black=16 inch). Amazingly, a black mark is visible on the black fleece. Cut out the circles with fabric scissors.

4. Sew target to white fabric. On the larger rectangle of white fabric, center the black circle and pin securely. Using black thread, stitch all the way around, as close as possible to the edge of the fleece.

Layer on the blue, red, and yellow circles and pin in place. Sew around each, working toward the yellow center. Continue to use black thread--it mostly disappears into the fuzziness of the fleece.

5. Sew the crash pad cover using French seams and envelope pillow back. Place the target face down on the ground and layer on the hemmed pieces right side up.

Overlap the hemmed edges approximately 6 inches in the center. The outside edges of the pillow front and back should be aligned. Pin the layers and stitch all the way around the edge with a scant 1/4 inch seam and white thread. Turn the pillow inside out, poking out the corners. Sew all the way around again, this time with approximately a 3/8 inch seam to fully encase the raw edges from the first seam. Turn the pillow right side out through the overlapped middle.

6. Cut foam. Depending on the size of foam scraps you acquired you will likely need to cut them up. A combination of cutting and tearing works well. Most pieces should be the size of a large fist but some can be larger.

7. Make interior pillow. Tear the muslin (or other fabric) into two rectangles 45 x 50 inches. Pin and stitch together around edges leaving an opening about 20 inches wide. Turn the pillow right side out and fill with foam chunks. After several uses the pillow will flatten so do fill it quite full. Fold in the raw edges of the opening, pin and stitch closed on sewing machine.

8. Slip the filled interior pillow into the target cover.

Pinning the final three layers of the target.

Chunks of foam ready to use-- note chiild's hand for scale.

CHEAPER

Collect old throw pillows and cushions to use for some of the stuffing.

Use old sheets, or a duvet cover, for the pillow fabric.

EASIER

Forego the target image. Purchase a heavy fabric from the home decorator section of the store and make the pillow, skipping steps 3 and 4.

Don't bother with the washable, removable cover at all. Just go to step 6 and use an attractive fabric.

FANCIER

If you have wood or tile floors you may want to secure a strip of rubber "footie pajama" fabric to the bottom of the pillow to reduce slipping. Do this in step 2 after hemming the edges of the pillow bottom.

Jack resting under a Heavy Blanket

Heavy Blanket

A heavy, or weighted blanket, is a very common recommendation made by occupational therapists for children who crave deep pressure input. Many children will enjoy wrapping themselves in this blanket when doing sedentary work activities like reading, writing, or watching TV. With this specific deep pressure input, their need to move decreases and their tolerance of light touch, various sounds, and visual distractions increases.

At bedtime, the Heavy Blanket may be a tool for children who need that extra input to relax and allow themselves to fall asleep. Regular bedsheets often produce light touch sensations during sleep, which can make for a restless night. If your child craves deep pressure but doesn't like the weight or finds it too warm, check out the Squeezy Sheets on page 80.

As described here, the finished blanket is 42 by 33 inches and weighs about 9 pounds. It can easily be made larger (or longer) for a bigger child or scaled down for a smaller child. The weight can also be adjusted. For a more portable lap weight, check out the Weighty Worm on page 30.

MATERIALS

Two yards of sturdy, 45 inch wide, quilting cotton, pre-washed

Approximately 9 pounds of poly pellets

1/3 cup measuring cup

Machine sewing supplies

Aim for your blanket to be approximately 10% of the user's body weight. For each 1/3 cup of pellets you can roughly calculate 1.5-2 ounces. But keep in mind that, unless the blanket is folded, a child's body will only be under a portion of the blanket at any given time so you can err a bit on the side of heavier.

Be certain that your child can easily move around under the blanket and independently remove it.

The blanket should wash up fine in a front loader machine--a top loader may not be ideal, as the friction of the agitator arm could pull the seams out of the weighted pockets.

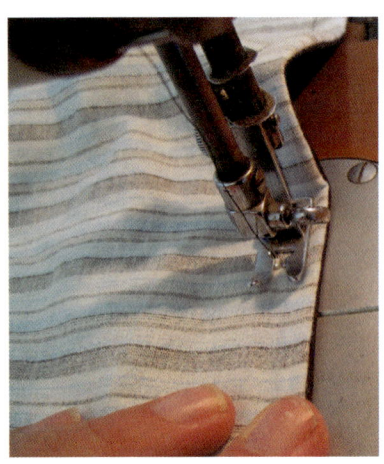

Sewing the French seam around three sides of the blanket

Marking the horizontal channel lines. Note that the vertical channels are already sewn from steps 2 and 3 not pictured.

The vertical channels are stitched and the horizontal rows are all marked. One end of the blanket remains completely open to insert poly pellets

1. Sew fabric case. Cut the fabric into two pieces of the same size (each approximately 45 x 36 inches). Pin with the wrong sides of the fabric together. Stitch along three edges using a scant 1/4 inch seam and leaving one 36 inch wide end open. Turn the blanket inside out and stitch again with a 3/8 inch seam to fully encase the first seam allowance on all three sides. This is what is called a French seam. Turn right side out again. It should be like an oversized pillow case approximately 44 x 33 inches.

2. Mark columns to hold poly pellets. Starting on one long side, make a mark every four inches along the bottom, narrow edge of the "pillowcase." Do the same along the top, open edge. If the width doesn't divide evenly by four, just widen/narrow a few columns--precision is not critical but the marks at the top and bottom should match up. Use the chalk or disappearing ink to draw vertical lines connecting the marks. You should have lines defining eight columns.

3. Sew columns. Pin the blanket together with pins within the vertical columns. Sew along each chalk line, creating eight vertical channels. Remove the pins.

4. Mark rows for poly pellets. Starting at the closed end of the blanket, mark a horizontal line in chalk every four inches. You are creating a 4 inch grid with the vertical columns you just sewed. The top row may be a bit wider or narrower than four inches and that's okay. You should have about 11 rows.

5. Begin filling channels and sewing the pockets closed. Pour 1/3 cup of poly pellets into each of the eight channels. As noted above, each 1/3 cup is approximately 1.5-2 ounces, so adjust the volume and weight as desired, taking care not to overfill the pockets. Shake the blanket to ensure the pellets are at the bottom. Now stitch across first horizontal chalk line.

This part can be tricky as the pellets want to leak up the channel and get under the needle. Use a pencil held flat and parallel to the stitch line to keep the pellets away from the needle. Go slowly--hitting a poly pellet will bend or break your needle. Another tip: This blanket is much easier to sew on a flat surface. If your machine is embedded in a table, great! If not, you may want to stack books around your sewing machine bed or use a machine quilting platform to reduce the pull on the needle.

Once the first horizontal seam is done, continue adding poly pellets to each channel and sewing across each row. For the final few rows, the pellets want to fall out. You may need to fill only a few columns at a time and pause frequently to fill the next columns.

4. Finish the top edge. Fill the final row with pellets and stitch across the top about one inch from the open edge to enclose the pellets. Fold over the raw edge twice and stitch it as if making a hem. Your blanket is done but the last step is to remove the lines you drew to create the grid. A quick spray of water will remove water soluble pen. For chalk, you can machine wash on the gentle or handwash cycle in a front loading machine.

Using the measuring cup to fill the channels working over a box to catch any spills.

Sewing the poly pellets into place. Note how the pencil keeps the pellets from getting under the needle.

CHEAPER

Recycle sturdy sheets for the fabric.

EASIER

Use standard, rather than French, seams for outside edges.

Make pockets larger and/or put fewer pellets in each pocket. This will result in a lighter blanket but it will be easier to sew.

FANCIER

Create a custom duvet cover (see the Texture Quilt on page 45 for ideas).

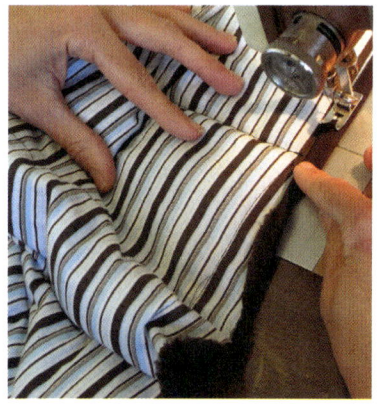

Hemming the end of the blanket to enclose the raw edge.

HEAVY STUFFED ANIMAL

Open a seam on a store bought stuffed animal and insert bean bags filled with poly pellets. This provides a nice weighted toy that can be carried around, placed in a backpack, or used as a lap buddy during sitting activities. Children who seek out proprioceptive input will enjoy the calming weight of this toy.

HEAVY BACKPACK

Using a weighted backpack can provide benefits similar to a weighted vest and can be used when headed to and from school to prepare the body for the demands of the day. Simply place heavy objects in the bottom of any backpack. Soft items like bean bags work well, but filled water bottles, a heavy book or even canned goods can provide necessary weight. As with the weighted blanket, be sure not to exceed 10% of the child's body weight.

42

CLASSROOM "SEAT BELT"

Choose a long piece of spandex, stretchy knit, or latex exercise band to tie around the leg of a chair. A fidgety child can use this to pull across their lap, over their shoulder, or around their hips. Many children find this pressure calming when sitting down to work or listen to a lesson. Let the child find the most comfortable and beneficial way to use the "belt." The tied off ends can can be used as a fidget to pull and stretch during quiet reading or while listening.

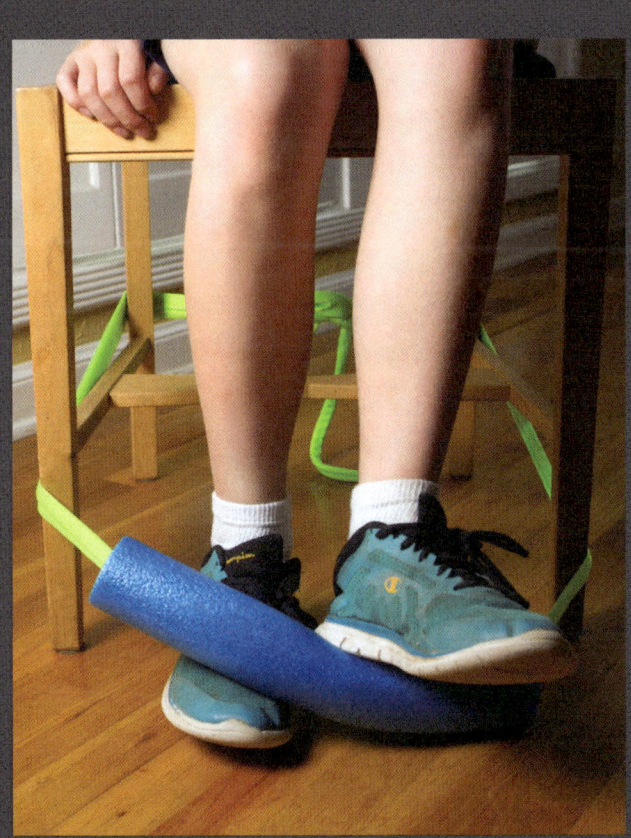

POOL NOODLE FOOT REST

Thread a length of Lycra through a cut-off piece of pool noodle and tie it to the legs of the desk chair. Children love to rest their feet on the pool noodle and use it like a fidget toy for their feet. It is very beneficial for those children who need movement to improve attention, as they can fidget with their foot rest without falling out of their chair or getting up multiple times during a lesson.

A bungee cord may also be used to attach the pool noodle to the chair but we had more success with the stretchy material.

Emery enjoying the Cocoon Swing.

Henry is a movement seeker and an extremely active grade schooler. Whenever he finds the opportunity, he's hanging from railings, off the edge of the bed, or over the back of the couch. He climbs everything in sight...then jumps off. Naturally he loves the playground, and anywhere he can be on the move with his feet off the ground. Since he was a toddler Henry has enjoyed swinging on the playground as high and as long as possible. He doesn't walk down the stairs, he jumps! It's hard for Henry to sit still and when required to sit, he rocks in his chair or finds excuses to get up frequently. His parents refer to him as having "ants in his pants."

Sophie is a three-year-old movement avoider who will not play on the playground equipment when she goes to the park with her friends. She likes to stand by her mother's side. When playing out of doors, she has difficulty with transitions on uneven surfaces, such as stepping off the curb into the mulched area or onto the grass from the sidewalk. She wants to hold her mother's hand as she walks around. Sophie does not mind being carried, but holds on quite tightly. If there are many children at the park, she will stand off to the side until she feels certain that she will not be knocked off balance by a passerby. Her mom refers to her as "clingy."

The vestibular system tells us where we are in relation to the earth based on receptors in our inner ear. Using our head position and the direction and speed of our movement through space, this system helps us maintain balance and control our eye movements. Deficits or delays in this complex system can have implications in many areas of development. Children can fall into two categories: movement seekers and movement avoiders. Both types have difficulty interpreting and responding to movement.

MOVEMENT SEEKERS are those children who seem to have a never-ending supply of energy. They keep going, and going. Even when they are sitting, they are in constant motion. These children may be mistaken for having attention deficit hyperactivity disorder (ADHD). Ask them to walk, and they might tell you they would prefer to run. These children enjoy moving because their vestibular systems under-register movement sensations. The more movement they get, the better able they are to make sense of their environment. Movement helps them improve postural responses, coordination and even their language skills. On the other hand, you may see this same child at school, melting into their chair, lying on the rug, or leaning into other people or objects for support. Their poorly developed postural responses prevent them from obtaining enough information to be able to maintain an adequate upright posture for independent sitting and standing.

MOVEMENT AVOIDERS are those kids who dislike being on uneven surfaces, have an aversion to having their feet off the ground (also known as gravitational insecurity), are unable to comfortably tilt their heads backward, and have difficulty tolerating movement. These children enjoy sedentary activities, as their bodies tend to overreact to vestibular input. They can become fearful when presented with a new movement challenge. Children with an intolerance to movement, or gravitational insecurity, tend to demonstrate many negative behaviors. These behaviors are rooted in true sensory dysregulation or sensory modulation disorder.

These projects can be used for both movement seekers and movement avoiders but the type of movement should be adapted to the child. Consult with a therapist to determine what types of movement would be best for your child.

CHARACTERISTICS TYPICAL OF A CHILD WITH VESTIBULAR SENSITIVITY

Movement Seeker

seeks movement or always on the go

no dizziness or nausea when swinging or spinning

fine motor difficulties

falls out of his chair

walks while talking

difficulty with complex motor tasks such as bike riding or shoe tying

Movement Avoider

resists putting head back in bath or shower

avoids lifting feet off ground

motion sickness

does not take movement risks, even with reassurance

uses handrail walking up and down stairs

does not alternate feet descending stairs

more emotionally sensitive than other children

maintains contact with parent or stable objects in the environment

In the vestibular chapter

Russell swinging in the Cocoon Swing.

Cocoon Swing

This super stretchy swing is perfect for children who like movement and proprioceptive input. And it's a lot of fun! The child who needs calming can curl up and relax with a favorite toy or book or stretch themselves out like a pencil. It is also a great tool to develop postural control when the child swings while lying on their stomach (Superman style). The setup of the swing can be easily adjusted to meet many different needs.

To use the swing, you'll need a very sturdy hanging rope, just as you would for a tire swing. Make sure the rope and hardware you use are appropriate for swings—check the weight rating of the rope and examine everything regularly for wear.

For indoor use (or even the garage), consult with a professional to ensure a ceiling hook is properly installed. For outdoor use, make sure to take the swing down and store it after each use. If the Lycra is constantly exposed to the elements it may break down more quickly.

Finally, this swing should be used with adult supervision and should be low to the ground or used with Target Crash Pillow or another soft landing underneath.

MATERIALS

2 yards of 58 inch wide Lycra or similar size

¼ yard of 60 inch wide midweight canvas fabric or denim

30 inch piece of 2 x 2 inch lumber

½ x 4 inch eye bolt with nut and two locking washers

~18 feet of sturdy rope (length depends on the height of the hook the swing will hang from)

Machine sewing supplies

Drill with ½ inch bit and a 1 inch forstner bit

Adjustable wrench

For this project I used ½ inch truck rope which fit perfectly in a ½ inch hole. Depending on your rope, you may need a slightly larger or smaller drill bit. The rope should fit snugly in the hole.

The 1 inch forstner bit is to countersink a hole for the hanging hardware. It's not critical but does reduce the likelihood of the child hitting their head on the bolt.

Fold and press the canvas to make the channels

Pin the "bias tape" over the long edges of the Lycra.

Sew "bias tape" in place. Note that the raw edge is folded under.

1. Create canvas channels. Cut the canvas into two 4.5 inch wide strips. Fold over ¼ inch on each side and press. Fold the strip in half and press again. The resulting strip should look like 2 inch wide double fold bias tape.

2. Sew swing. Fold the Lycra in half so it is 36 x 58 inches. It's slippery so pin the layers. Pin the canvas "bias tape" along each 58 inch long edge securing the raw edges and folded edge of the Lycra inside the canvas. At each end, fold under the raw edge of the bias tape to hide cut edges. Stitch the layers together as close as possible to the edge of the bias tape. Stitch again so you have two parallel seams for extra security. This step leaves a channel inside the canvas along each side of the swing.

3. Build the swing top. On the 2 x 2 lumber, starting at one end, mark dots at 2 inches, 5 inches, 15 inches, 25 inches and 28 inches. At each dot drill through the center of the lumber with a ½ inch drill bit. On the center hole, drill a ½ inch deep countersink on one side. Thread a locking washer on the eye bolt and put it through the center hole toward the countersink. Thread on another locking washer and then the nut which should go into the countersink. Tighten with a wrench.

4. Assemble the swing. Cut the rope in half to make two 9 foot pieces. If it's synthetic rope, melt the ends to keep them from unraveling. Thread one rope through one channel on the swing and the other rope through the other channel. Thread the rope through the wood up toward the top of the eye bolt. The swing can be arranged so the channels on the Lycra are parallel to the wood or perpendicular. Knot the rope above the wood to secure it and adjust the height of the knots to raise or lower the swing. You may need to spend some time adjusting the swing position to best suit your setup and your child.

5. Hang the swing by attaching the eyebolt to a hanging rope. You may need to use a climbing grade carabiner to make it easy to take the swing down when it's not in use.

CHEAPER

Use recycled materials such as denim jeans for the canvas.

Use a very sturdy branch for the wood.

The most expensive part of the project, by far, is the Lycra, which is critical. Be sure to use a coupon at your local big box fabric store.

EASIER

Instead of using a bar above the swing, thread the rope through the channels and hang the swing between two trees like a hammock. Again, the channels can be perpendicular or parallel to the line between the trees.

Instead of using a piece of wood, simply thread ropes through the channels and tie the ropes to the hanging device.

Purchase more Lycra and simply tie the corners of the Lycra to a hanging device.

FANCIER

Add layers of Lycra—instead of two layers do three or four. This makes a sturdier swing for heavier children or, allows children to climb between the layers for additional proprioceptive input and to practice motor planning skills.

Use a double row of stitching to secure the "bias tape" channel to the Lycra.

The eye bolt is centered on the wood and the nut on the bottom is in the receccessed area.

One way to arrange the ropes and swing. Note that the knots above the wood are adjustable.

Noah balancing on the Rocker Board.

Rocker Board

Postural control and balance are foundational for the development of focus, attention, and organization of the body and mind. A rocker board can be used as a fun toy, as a tool for developing muscle strength and control, or as an activity to promote balance and body aware-ness.

The materials for the rocker board can be found at any Home Depot or other home center.

Do not use the rocker board indoors on wood floors—it could scratch or dent them!

MATERIALS

18 inch round table top

18 inch piece of stair handrail (as long as your top is wide)

5 wood screws, 2 inches long

Saw, if needed to cut down length of wood or handrail

Cordless drill/driver

1/8 inch drill bit with a counter-tersink or a small bit plus a ¼ inch bit to create counter-sink

Driver bit (Phillips head)

Ruler or straight edge

Stair handrail is found in the molding section of the home center. It will look like an approximately 2 inch wide dowel with one side sliced off to form a flat edge.

If you don't want to buy wood or a handrail that is longer than you need, it can be sawed off for you at the home improvement center.

Mark the center of the table top.

Position hand rail. Note that the line extends around the edge.

Drill pilot holes then screw top to handrail.

1. Draw a line across the center of the round table top perpendicular to the grain. Continue the line around the edge of the wood and across the underside. Hold (or tape) the handrail piece on the bottom of the wood centered on the pencil line.

2. Drill through the top and into the handrail with the small bit, evenly spacing the holes across the width. Create a shallow divot that is about ¼ inch wide as a countersink so the screw head will be flush with the surface of the rocker.

3. Drive screws through rocker and into the handrail piece to secure.

CHEAPER

Options for the top include: 18-24 inch length of 12 inch wide lumber, square of sturdy chip board, or any other flat, sturdy piece of wood at least 12 x 18 inches. Look for recycled lumber.

FANCIER

Paint it! This is especially fun to do with your child. For durability, spray or brush on a clear coat finish over the paint.

Due to the nature of the vestibular system the super simple projects in this chapter don't require any making at all. Getting outside and repurposing household items are great ways to support the vestibular system.

Charlie enjoys the Sawyer Swing.

Sawyer Swing

Swings are a favorite for many children! Movement seekers love the vestibular input that swinging provides. There are two swing patterns in this book to address the needs of many children. The Cocoon Swing (see page 49) is great for calming, but for those who prefer rough and tumble play, the Sawyer Swing is a fun option. It's sturdy and versatile and a great project to make with your child. This swing allows for rotational input and, depending how it is constructed, can promote balance and core strength as both are needed to keep the platform stable.

MATERIALS

12 foot long piece of 2 x 4 lumber

Many feet of very sturdy rope

20 two inch long wood screws

Climbing grade carabiner

Saw

Screwdriver or cordless driver

Drill with 1/8 inch bit and large bit (approximately 5/8 inch)

Check the maximum load rating on the rope and purchase the sturdiest you can find. The rope length will depend on where your swing will be hung.

Measure from the hanging location to the ground and purchase four times that length plus two feet. So, if your swing will hang from a rope dangling nine feet off the ground, purchase 38 feet of rope (9 x 4 plus 2). You can always trim the rope but you don't want to be caught short.

EASIER

Use a thick piece of plywood or a wood disc (as in the rocker board project) instead of the 2 x 4s to make the swing platform.

FANCIER

Before attaching the rope, stain or paint the 2 x 4s for a more finished look. Be sure your lumber is dry before adding stain or paint.

The small holes are drilled and the upper boards are screwed the lower boards. Note that the holes near the edges are out of line to allow space for the large hole for the rope.

Melt the ends of synthetic rope to prevent fraying.

Knot the rope underneath the platform. Note how boards are arranged.

1. **Saw the 2 x 4 board** into seven 20 inch long pieces.

2. **Lay two boards approximately 13 inches apart** and lay the five remaining boards across them, spaced evenly across the 20 inch width of the swing. Line up the ends of the five boards with the outer edge of the bottom board.

3. **Drill two pilot holes** with the 1/8 inch drill bit in both ends of each top board through into the bottom boards. Secure using screws. Be sure the screws at corners do not interfere with where you will need to drill the hole for the rope in step 4.

4. **Use a large drill** bit to drill all the way through both 2 x 4s approximately 1.5 inches in from each corner. The drill bit should be the same diameter as your rope (approximately 5/8 inch).

5. **Cut rope into two even pieces.** For synthetic rope, melt the ends to prevent fraying. Twist the rope to squeeze it through the hole from top to bottom. Make a tight knot on the bottom of the swing. Put the other end of the same rope into the other hole on the same side of the swing. Repeat with the second rope so the ropes make triangles above the swing platform.

6. **It's time to hang your swing.** This swing is best hung low to the ground. The perfect height would allow the child to mount the swing independently and yet still be high enough that it does not touch the ground when swinging. This comes out to approximately 8-12 inches off the ground. Hook the ropes through the carabiner and check the height. The knots

below the swing can be adjusted to raise the swing. You may also want to make knots at the top of the rope. These directions allow the swing to tip front to back to promote balance and core strength.

Note that the rope is looped over the carabiner. It can also be knotted for additional stability.

BALL CHAIR

A large, bouncy ball or a small yoga ball makes a perfect seat for a small, wiggly child. A child who seeks movement when working may benefit from constant postural adjustments that sitting on this uneven surface allows. Continuously activating the child's trunk muscles throughout the task will channel that need for movement in a positive way, increasing focus, and improving postural control.

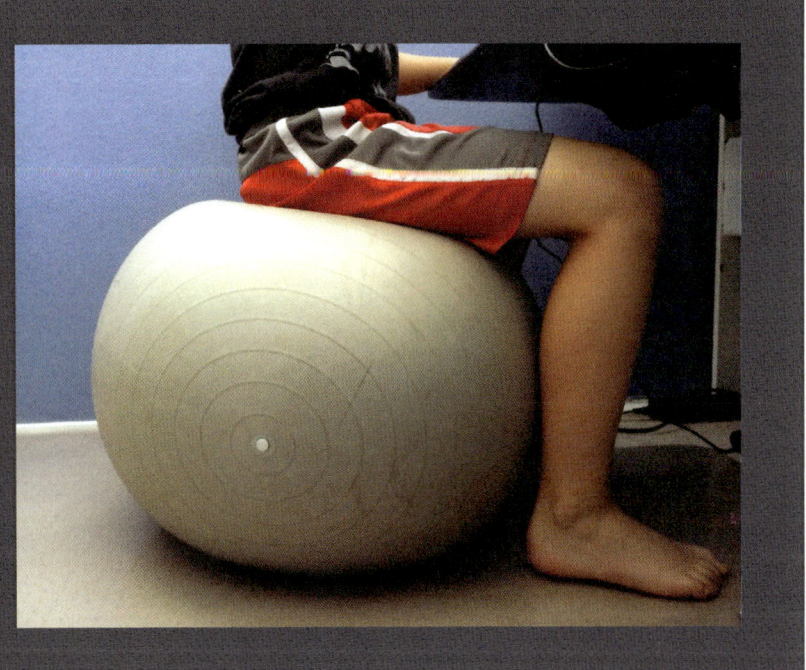

SPINNING CHAIR

If your child enjoys spinning in circles, in swings or on other playground equipment, find a second-hand office chair and let them spin at home. This a simple, home-based alternative, and works well when the weather does not allow for a trip the swings. Kids who need rotational input will likely seek it out so you may as well designate a sturdy chair. Allow the child to guide this activity. Therapeutic rotational input should never be imposed on a child without proper supervision from a trained therapist as negative reactions may occur (nausea, dizziness, vomiting, mood changes, low blood pressure, and others).

Jay works while seated on a One-legged Stool.

One-legged Stool

Many children need to move to learn. A one-legged stool is an alternative seating method that allows for small amounts of movement while seated and working at a table. It engages the muscles required for sitting and reduces a child's need to fidget. This movement (using the stool) can work to improve body awareness, balance and coordination, as well as promote perceptual motor skill development.

MATERIALS

1 inch galvanized "nipple" pipe approximately 12 inches long

1 inch floor flange

8 inch piece of 2 x 6 wood (or other, similar sized wood scrap)

one 1¼ inch rubber tip

four 1 inch screws

Sandpaper (electric sander is nice but not required)

Drill and bits

Screwdriver

Note that pipe width (that is, diameter) is measured by interior dimension.

Pipe length will depend on the height of the child but a 12 inch pipe with a 2 inch thick seat is the proper height for children approximately age 9-11. At my local hardware store pipe comes precut in 12 and 15 inch lengths but can be cut to size. If you have the pipe cut, be sure to retain one threaded end. The stool should be sized so that the seated child can have his feet flat on the floor and have knees and hips at 90 degrees.

Supplies. Note that wood is sanded.

Mark the location to drill pilot holes.

Drill the pilot holes.

Screw on the flange then screw in the pipe. Note the rubber tip.

1. Sand the wood piece and round the edges with a sander.

2. Center the floor flange on the wood piece and use a pencil to mark the location of the screw holes.

3. Drill pilot holes on the marks with a drill bit slightly smaller than the screws.

4. Screw the floor flange in place on the piece of wood.

5. Screw the pipe into the floor flange. Put the rubber tip on the end of the pipe to protect the floor during use.

To mount the stool, have your child stand with their feet shoulder-width apart. They should reach back to steady the stool on the ground behind them with both hands and sit slowly on the stool to prevent the stool from sliding out from under them. The child's hips, knees and ankles should be at a 90-degree angle when sitting. This stool can be used to replace a chair at a table or as an alternative to floor sitting.

CHEAPER

If the pipe comes with a cover on the threaded end and your floors aren't precious, skip the rubber cover.

Seek out scrap or recycled wood pieces for the seat.

FANCIER

Paint the wooden seat with your child.

Adjust the height of the chair by using thicker or thinner wood for the seat top.

SCOOTERBOARD

A scooterboard is a fun toy that provides linear movement in small spaces. You can ride it on your tummy down the hallway or pull yourself across the living room with a rope. The proprioceptive input from propelling the scooter calms the body while the movement provides the vestibular input. There are many other therapeutic uses for a scooterboard -- upper body strengthening, bilateral coordination, and postural control. To create your own scooterboard, you can get a sturdy piece of wood large enough for a child to sit or lie on comfortably and attach casters. Add fabric covered foam or carpet to make it a bit fancier. You can also use a car-repair creeper or a trash can dolly for a ready-made alternative.

HEAD TO THE PLAYGROUND

Set aside time to play at the local park or playground. Playground equipment provides many opportunities for vestibular input. For linear input, swing in the standard swings. If your playground has a tire swing, that is great for rotational movement. Slides provide opportunities for linear movement and proprioceptive input as you ascend the ladder or climb up the slide itself. Monkey bars provide both linear movement, proprioceptive input, and upper body strengthening. Move over to the grassy field to wrestle, play kickball, log roll down a gentle hill, or twirl in circles. There are many fantastic ways to promote the integration of the vestibular sense at the playground!

TRICKS FOR MOVEMENT AVOIDERS

When children get overstimulated by vestibular input, there are a couple tricks that may help resolve that underlying motion sick feeling. These tricks can be used for those who become car sick as well.
- Hard jumping on a firm surface
- Warhead Super Sour Spray
- True Lemon - unsweetened crystalized lemon packets
- Sour candies such as Sour Patch Kids, Warheads, Lemonheads

Shelby and Colby explore the contents of some Fidget Bags

Jared is a four year-old boy who has a lot of trouble interpreting tactile information. His mother has to cut his hair while he is sleeping, over the course of two to three nights. He needs to be restrained to have his fingernails or toenails trimmed. Jared refuses to wear shoes and prefers to wear his shirts inside out or backward, because the tags bother his neck.

When gently touched by another person or object, he vigorously rubs that spot on his body as though he is rubbing out the sensation. Any unexpected touch causes a fight-or-flight reaction. He jumps back in alarm when his mom gently touches his shoulder to guide him through the busy store. He does not yet know how to make sense of those unexpected or unfamiliar touch sensations.

On the flip side, Jared can't keep his hands off of anything, even Grandma's breakable figurines. He runs his hands along the walls and furniture as he navigates his home or classroom. He fidgets with any object within reach. He is a boy trying to make sense of everything by imposing touch on his own terms.

The sense of touch is one of the most basic senses and is the first to develop in utero. The sensory system is the largest in our bodies and takes in an enormous amount of information. There are many kinds of touch sensations, both internal and external: light touch, deep pressure, vibration, temperature, and pain. How individuals interpret this information can give them important, information about their environment as well as protect them from harm. The body uses a neural process called inhibition to determine which tactile input is important.

Children who have difficulty interpreting tactile input may seek out more input than others (hyposensitivity), avoid unfamiliar touch sensations (hypersensitivity), or have strong negative reactions to unexpected or seemingly benign touch sensations (defensiveness).

As with most sensory systems, sensitivity to touch falls along a spectrum. Tactile hypersensitivity can be seen with children who are easily irritated by tactile input that would not bother most people and this sensitivity may impact day to day behaviors. Tactile defensiveness refers to a set of symptoms that include strong negative reactions (physically and emotionally) to many kinds of tactile input. For those with defensiveness, tactile experiences often trigger a fight-or-flight response and many negative behavioral reactions, such as avoidance behaviors. This can significantly impact a child's social and emotional well-being.

Tactile hyposensitivity is when an individual needs more touch input for the sensation to be perceived. In order for them to make sense of the world, they seek out various touch sensations in the world around them.

CHARACTERISTICS TYPICAL OF A CHILD WITH TACTILE SENSITIVITY

Tactile Hypersensitivity and Defensiveness

upset during grooming activities

withdraws from touch

low pain tolerance

avoids getting messy

wants to wash messes off body

"rubs out" light touch sensations

easily bothered by clothing items

Tactile Hyposensitivity

doesn't notice messy hands or face

prefers clothes and shoes that are too tight

frequently touches things

enjoys walking barefoot

takes very hot showers without being bothered

wears clothing inappropriate for the weather

In the tactile chapter

Texture Quilt
Page 68

Fidget Bag
Page 72

Marble Maze
Page 76

Squeezy Sheets
Page 80

Super Simple Projects
Page 79, 83-85

Casey explores the different fabrics of the Texture Quilt.

Texture Quilt

The Texture Quilt is a perfect snuggling object for children who seek out tactile input. It's especially great paired with the Heavy Blanket. (see page 38) For children who enjoy feeling different textures, this can be a useful outlet for obtaining those needed sensations. It can provide a sense of calm. A smaller version can be used as a lap pad for those who need something to fidget with in the classroom. The key to this project is to choose a wide variety of textures so children can feel preferred textures but also challenge themselves with less-preferred textures.

These directions are for an approximately 44 x 54 inch lap quilt but can easily be sized up or down.

To reduce visual sensory input, consider buying all fabrics in the same basic color. This can be challenging for utility fabrics which are often white so another option is to purchase all white fabrics and overdye the finished quilt so dirt and stains aren't as obvious.

MATERIALS

Scraps of ten different textured fabrics. Each scrap should be at least 4.5 x 6.5 inches.

Wide satin blanket binding (two packages)

1.5 yards of 45 inch wide fabric for quilt back (quilting cotton, flannel or minky are perfect)

1.5 yards of 45 inch wide fabric for front (woven cotton or flannel)

3 yards 45 inch wide flannel (or a flat flannel sheet) for batting

Machine sewing supplies

Natural fibers: silk, linen, wool, cottons: flannel, chenille, seersucker, corduroy

Synthetics: "silky" polyester, fleece, minky, faux fur, velour, embellished fashion fabrics

Utility fabrics: pajama feet fabric (has little rubber nubs on cotton), terry cloth, nylon (as used for outdoor gear)

Upholstery fabrics: textured brocades

Wander your local big box fabric store feeling the fabrics and choose a selection of soft, rough, bumpy, furry, and other textures. Also look for scraps and samples of fabrics and consider repurposing fabrics you have around your home such as old sheets and towels, or outgrown pajamas.

Make sure any fabric you choose is washable! Burlap, for example, has a great texture but is not washable and should not be used. Pre-wash all fabrics (especially wools and furs) to ensure washability and that they have shrunk before you begin.

Textured fabrics.

Cut textured pieces to size with a rotary cutter or scissors.

Packaged satin blanket binding shown on finished quilt.

1. Cut your top fabric. Ensure your fabric is square then measure down 12 inches from the top edge of the top fabric and cut the fabric in half from selvedge to selvedge. Measure down five more inches and cut off a strip that is five inches wide. Tearing works well for woven fabrics.

2. Assemble the texture strip. Cut each textured fabric into a 4.5 x 6.5 inch rectangle. Also cut two rectangles from the strip you just cut out of the top fabric. Sew the long edges of the pieces together with a ¼ inch seam to create a strip 6.5 inches tall and approximately 48.5 inches long. The rectangles made from the top fabric should be at each end of the strip. This ensures the quilt binding won't cover any of the texture patches.

3. Sew in the texture strip. Center the texture strip on the 12 inch wide strip of top fabric. Sew the edges with good sides together. Trim the ends of the texture strip even with the edges of the top fabric. Sew the longer piece of front fabric to the bottom of the texture strip. Iron seams as needed but be careful not to scorch or melt synthetic fabrics!

4. Make a quilt sandwich. Layer the quilt back wrong side up, two layers of flannel (or flannel sheet) and quilt top good side up. Don't worry if the flannel is oversized but do line up two edges to ensure the back fabric is directly underneath the top fabric.

5. Pin and sew. Pin all four layers together. Then topstitch through all four layers along the top and bottom of the texture strip and around the edge of the entire quilt. Trim excess flannel from the edges.

6. Add satin binding. With the right side of the quilt up, wrap the binding around the quilt, covering the outer 2 inches of quilt with the satin. Start sewing approximately 2 inches from the finished edge of the satin binding.

Using a wide zigzag stitch and coordinating thread zigzag close to the edge of the satin, making certain you are always catching the satin on the back of the quilt. At the corners, stop sewing about 3 inches from the corner and plant the needle. Turn the fabric at the outer corner and tuck the triangles of binding in on both sides. Pin in place. Stitch to the inside of the corner, zig zag out to the outer corner and back in.

Check the back to ensure all the satin binding is secured before continuing down the next side. When one package of binding runs out, overlap the next package and sew out to the edge and back down before proceeding. At the end, stop and plant the needle about 3 inches before you reach the loose end of binding where you started. Cut off the binding so that 1.5 inches goes under the start of the binding. You want the cut end under the factory end so it doesn't unravel. Pin and sew in place. Backstitch to secure the end of the stitch line.

For a visual demonstration of securing satin binding, watch the video available on YouTube via DIYSuperToys.com.

CHEAPER

Use as many recycled materials as possible, including thrift store sheets for the back and interior.

Skip the satin binding—it's quite expensive—and finish the quilt edges with cotton quilt binding or in another manner.

EASIER

Use fewer different texture fabrics—just adjust the size of each piece to make up the quilt width.

FANCIER

Instead of a quilt, make a duvet cover to go over the weighted blanket.

Use any traditional quilt pattern but instead of printed calicoes use textured fabric for the different parts of the quilt.

Add yarn ties to further secure the layers of the quilt. The yarn ties will be a fidget item for the child.

Overdye the completed quilt with fabric dye. Note that different types of fabrics will take dye differently. Synthetic fabrics (like polyester fleece) may not change color at all while cottons and natural fibers typically take dye well. The color variation is part of the fun.

The texture strip is sewn in place and the quilt sandwich is made with plaid flannel sheet "batting."

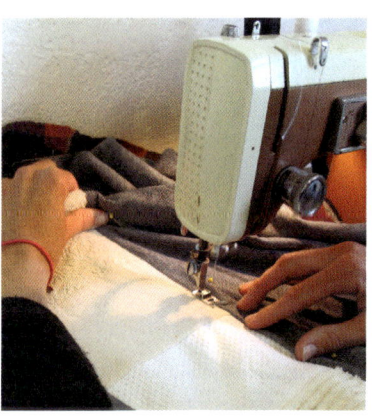

Quilting along the edge of the texture strip.

Example of a texture quilt made by improvisationally piecing textured fabrics.

Emery looks for something to play with in the Fidget Bag.

Fidget Bag

A Fidget Bag helps children self-soothe and is particularly useful in environments where children need to be still and quiet. Almost anything can be fun in a fidget bag but the best items are those that are easily manipulated in one hand, quiet, and personalized to the child's preferences (toy car, personal objects, favorite colors).

These directions are for a small bag and items to include but this project is endlessly adaptable and the internet is filled with fidget ideas.

We created one "traditional" fidget bag with a mix of handmade and dollar store items and a "nature" fidget bag filled with collected, natural treasures.

For children who have difficulty with tactile discrimination this project can also be used to play a game called What's in the Bag?. Fill the bag with 10-12 familiar objects that have different shapes, sizes, weights and textures (i.e., paper clip, pencil, eraser, marble, cotton ball, Lego brick, rubber band, sponge, playing card, plastic lid, spoon). Have your child identify each item as they feel it without looking in. To make it easier, ask them to feel for a specific item. To make it harder, have items in the bag with similar attributes.

MATERIALS

Scraps of fabric, four pieces, each at least 8.5 x 10 inches.

60 inches of approximately 3/8 inch wide ribbon or twill tape

Machine sewing supplies

Awesome fidgets--see lists on the next page

Quilting cotton works great, but you can use almost any fabric. Or use a piece of patchwork or decorated fabric.

Sew top edges of lining pieces to outside pieces.

Mark 3/4 inch gaps on outer fabric 1/2 inch below seam connecting lining and outside fabric.

Pin and sew leaving gaps open.

1. Cut the fabric into four rectangles, each 8.5 x 10 inches. Two rectangles will be the lining of the bag and two will be the outside of the bag.

2. Sew top edges. Put one lining piece and one outer piece good sides together and sew along one 8.5 inch edge with a ¼ inch seam. (If your fabric is directional, this seam will be the top of the bag.) Repeat for other piece of lining and outer.

3. Sew bag pieces. Open the sewn pieces so the seam is in the middle of a long rectangle. Stack the pieces on top of each other with good sides together. The lining should be on top of lining and outer on top of outer. The seams sewn in step 2 should be on top of each other. Pin around the edges.

4. Mark gaps to leave open. Leave a 2 inch gap at the bottom of the lining pieces and ¾ inch gaps on the outer pieces ½ inch below the middle seam.

5. Sew around outside edge with a ¼ inch seam, skipping over the marked gaps. Be sure to lock the stitches with a bit of forward and backward stitching on each side of the gaps.

7. Turn the piece right side out through the hole in the bottom of the lining. Sew the hole closed.

8. Push the lining fabric into the outer fabric and press. Top stitch approximately ½ inch from the top of the bag all the way around the top. This seam should be at the top of the gap in the outer fabric. Top stitch again below the gap in side seam, approximately 1.25 inches from the top edge of the bag.

9. Insert drawstrings. Cut the ribbon into two 30-inch pieces. Using a blunt needle or safety pin, thread one ribbon through one hole in the outer fabric all around the bag and out the same hole. Repeat this procedure starting on the other side with the other ribbon. Knot the ribbons on each side. When you pull on the knots it will draw the bag closed.

10. Fill with fidgets!

Kids who need to squish and squeeze

rubbery, non-messy toy such as Silly Putty

Fidget Balloons (see page 83)

foam stress balls

Kids who like to pick and peel

corks

sticky notes

tape flags such as Post-it tape

Kids who need to keep fingers busy

Marble Maze (see page 76)

pompoms

paperclips

rubber band ball

rings

pipe cleaners

spring toys like Slinky

Oral fidgets

plastic spiral key rings

beaded necklace or bracelet, provided the beads will not pop off easily

gum, hard candies, or lollipops

aquarium tubing on top of pencil (see page103)

The baby and pet sections of stores have inexpensive items that make surprisingly good fidgets.

Fidgets from nature

acorns and acorn tops

sticks or driftwood

wool yarn wrapped around a stick

worry stone made of a river rock or other smooth stone

shells or coral (not too sharp!)

seed pods

wool or wool covered stones (see page 85)

This is how it will look once turned inside out.

Insert drawstrings into opening in outer fabric.

CHEAPER

Use recycled fabric from sheets or shirts for bag.

Make fidgets (such as yarn pom poms) or buy second hand.

EASIER

Use a pre-made bag or small box.

FANCIER

Add texture to bag exterior (see Texture Quilt on page 68 for ideas).

Write the child's name in slick paint or embroider it for added textural interest.

Add tassels or pom poms to the tie.

75

Carlos pushes the marble through the Marble Maze.

Marble Maze

This simple project is fun for many children. The Marble Maze can be used as a fidget for those children who need to keep their hands busy. It can also be used as a finger strengthening activity for those with delays in fine motor development, motor coordination, and visual perceptual skills. And, it can also be used as a calming tool, as the act of pushing the marble through the resistive material provides proprioceptive feedback to the fingers.

MATERIALS

Fleece scraps, two pieces, each at least 6.5 x 9 inches (¼ yard of fleece is plenty)

Small marble (approximately ½ inch in diameter)

Machine sewing supplies

This pattern can be made with a variety of fabrics, though something with a bit of stretch is easier.

The width of the channels between the rows of stitching may need to be adjusted depending on your fabric and the size of your marble. Before sewing the entire project, stack two scraps of your fabric and stitch parallel lines ¾ inch apart. Insert your marble and make sure your marble fits snugly in the channel. If it's too loose or too snug, adjust the ¾ inch channel width and use your custom channel width in the directions that follow.

Mark the lines in chalk.

Areas to be left open are marked with a cross hatch.

Sew along chalk lines skipping the areas to be left open.

1. Cut two rectangles of fleece, each 6.5 x 9 inches. Of course, this size isn't magic. This project can be any size you wish—feel free to adapt it to your needs.

2. Draw a line with the chalk pencil that is parallel to, and 1 inch away from, a long edge. Measure over ¾ inches and draw another line. Continue so you have parallel chalk lines every ¾ inches across the fleece (allowing at least 1 inch on each edge).

3. Mark openings. In each line, mark with chalk one or two spots which will be openings in the maze. The openings should be at least ¾ inch wide. Pin layers together.

4. Sew along the interior lines being careful to leave the openings open. Do a bit of forward and backstitching at the openings and the beginning and end of each line to secure the threads.

5. Sew the edges but don't forget the marble! Once the interior lines are sewn, slide a marble into one of the channels and sew around the entire maze with a scant ¼ inch seam. Trim all the threads.

CHEAPER

It may not be cheaper but instead of a marble it may be easier to find a ball bearing at a local hardware store, or a decorative glass bead (used in vases), or other type of bead etc.

Use scrap fabric. Be aware that fleece is quite stretchy so be sure to test the channel width with other fabrics. An old sweatshirt or heavy t-shirt would work well.

FANCIER

Make a more complicated maze pattern or a spiral labyrinth.

Put two marbles in the maze.

Embroider the fabric or add a decorative blanket stitch to the edge.

OOBLECK

Mix equal parts cornstarch and water. Add a drop of food coloring and let the fun begin. The resulting mixture is solid when squeezed and liquid when released. Your sensory-seeking child (and you) can be entertained for quite a while as this provides proprioceptive input as you dig through the solid form for hidden objects, swish your fingers through to practice color mixing, and let it ooze through your fingers to get that wet, messy sensation. It cleans up fairly easily with water or can be dusted off surfaces once dry.

GEL IN A BAG

Fill a zipper freezer bag about 1/3 full with hair gel (check your local dollar store for the gel). Add some sequins, glitter, or shaped metallic confetti from your child's last birthday party and/or a couple drops of food coloring for a personal touch. Press out the air and secure the zipper. Cover the zipper with folded duct tape then a second layer of duct tape. The gel bag is fun to squish and can also be smoothed flat and used as a drawing surface for practicing letter forms.

Jay rests under a squeezy sheet.

Squeezy Sheets

For many children with tactile sensitivities, the light touch sensation of clothing and sheets can be distressing and uncomfortable. Often times, using a heavy blanket is not an option, for example in warm weather or if the child is too small to safely use a weighted blanket. Squeezy sheets replace the top sheet on the bed and provide firm pressure input while lounging or sleeping. The amount of pressure can be adjusted to meet your child's unique needs.

This is a very simple, no-sew project. The most important thing is to purchase extremely stretchy knit fabric.

MATERIALS

For a twin size mattress

2 yards very stretchy knit fabric is enough for a twin size mattress

The squeezy sheet will be as long as the knit fabric is wide. So a 54 inch wide fabric will yield a 54 inch long sheet. For taller children, purchase the widest possible fabric.

Choose a knit that stretches in both directions (along length and width). Ideally, find something almost as stretchy as lycra or dancewear fabric but thicker and made of a cotton blend. For the fabric I used, a 10 inch square of fabric could be stretched to 24 inches in one direction and 19 inches in the other direction and still return to the original 10 inches. If you are able, go to the store and stretch the knits you find.

Big box stores may carry what you need; mill end or remnant stores can also be a good source for knit. Printed knits from the children's section of a big box store are unlikely to be stretchy enough and many of the "fashion" knits are too lightweight. Look for something the weight of a high quality, heavyweight t-shirt but much, much stretchier. I had the best luck at a mill end/remnant store.

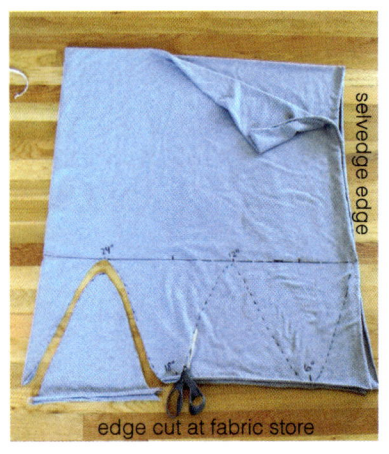

Cut diagram.

The shape of the cut fabric.

Tie on the squeezy sheet.

1. Fold the fabric in half matching the cut ends of the fabric. The resulting rectangle should be 36 inches tall and as wide as your fabric was wide (i.e., 54 inches). Fold in half again again bringing selvedges together and keeping the cut edges aligned.

2. Measure 12 inches from the cut edge and make a line across the fabric parallel to the cut edge.

3. Mark for cutting. Along the cut edge and starting at the selvedge edge, measure in 6 inches and make a mark. Measure 12 more inches and make another mark. Along the line drawn in step two, measure in 12 inches from the selvedge edge and make a mark. Measure 12 more inches and make another mark. If your measurements don't line up precisely with the width of your fabric, don't worry. The main goal is to have two and a half bumps along the cut edge, precision isn't critical.

4. Freehand cut the fabric in a wave pattern connecting marks as shown.

5. Tie the squeezy sheet to the mattress over the fitted sheet and in lieu of the top sheet. It can be tied tighter or looser to match the child's preferences.

CHEAPER

Mill end and remnant stores often have inexpensive knit fabrics—see if there is such a store in your town.

FANCIER

Paint or dye the fabric—tie dye would be fun.

FIDGET BALLOONS

Blow up 12 inch party balloons a few times to stretch them and then use a funnel to fill them. Different fillings result in different sensory experiences. Try: sand, flour, cornstarch, rice or beans, poly pellets, hair gel and more. After filling the balloon as much as possible make a knot. And then put it inside another balloon for added durability. If the balloon gets a hole it's just time to make more!

PLAY BINS

Use shoebox size plastic containers. Fill with various tactile media (rice, beans, sand, shaving cream, salt, pebbles, Easter grass, sawdust, etc.) and hide objects inside to find. You can have a different tub for each month or holiday!

STICKY DESK

A strip of double stick tape or adhesive backed Velcro under the edge of the desk or table helps kids who need tactile input in order to work quietly at their desk. It is a fidget that can't go flying across the room or get lost.

NUBBY WASH CLOTHS

Textured washcloths can help make bath time more pleasurable. Kids who seek out touch sensations will enjoy the added input of a nubby or rough wash mitt. Look for a microfiber "chenille" mitt often suggested for dusting. If your child doesn't like that sensation, try tulle "poufs" or exfoliating scrub cloths, or anything else your child might enjoy.

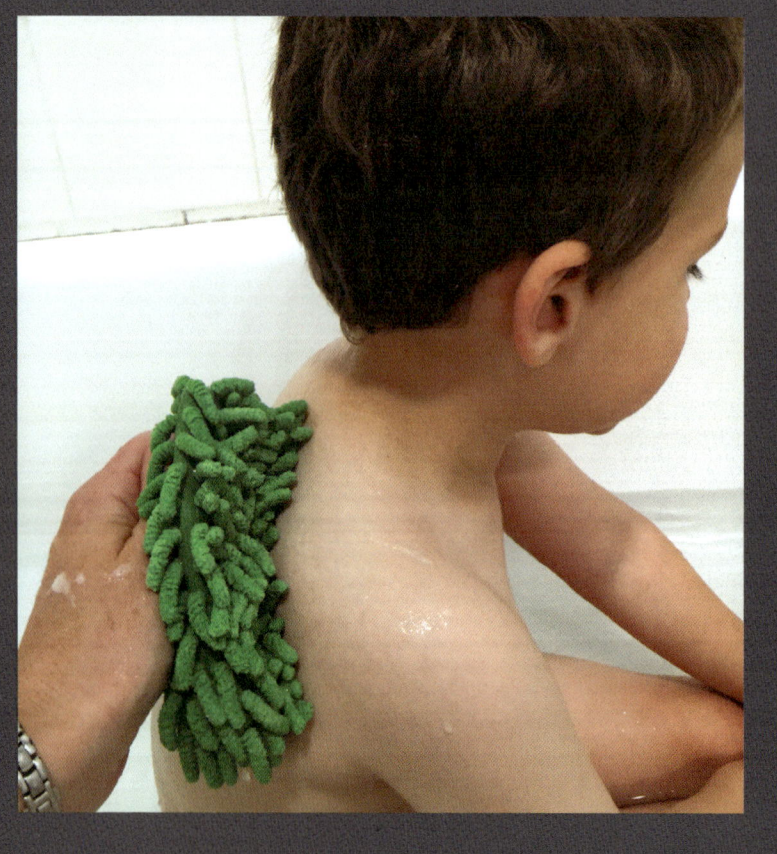

WOOL STONES

Gather small (1-2 inch diameter) stones and purchase wool roving (sold at yarn shops for felting or spinning). Tightly wrap 2 or more feet of wool roving around each stone, changing directions frequently. Holding the wrapped stone in your fist, shove it into the toe of an old pair of nylon stockings. Knot the stockings and add another stone. Once the stocking is full, and looks like sausage links, wash the stone stockings in the washing machine with a load of towels and hot water. Peel the felted stones out of the stockings and allow to air dry. These are great for a fidget bag. For more detailed instructions, check out DIYSuperToys.com

BEADED TREASURES

Add pony beads or perler beads to a shoelace, piece of yarn, or embroidery floss. A longer length can be tied into a long necklace. A shorter length can be a bracelet, anklet, or a hand fidget. If you leave room for the beads to move, it makes a perfect finger fidget. This is a great tool to use when kids are sitting on the rug and need to keep their hands occupied! Some children prefer to have a small piece of pipe cleaner accessible that they can add or remove beads. This is best for a desk fidget for older children who are able to safely manage any loose beads.

other senses
auditory, visual, oral, & olfactory

Jack chewing on an Aquarium Tube Pencil Topper.

Clara is a first grader who doesn't seem aware that her voice is too loud for certain situations. She also has been observed chewing holes in the sleeves and neckline of her shirts. She asks her mother to buy sweaters with zippers so she has something to chew, and often her clothing is wet down the front by lunchtime. Though she has since dropped the habit, she used to lick the mirror because, she says, " I liked how it felt." For as much as Clara enjoys oral sensory input, she can be easily set off by smells. For example, she can not tolerate the smell of her friend's shampoo. She asks to leave the room if someone is wearing body spray or perfume, even if they are far away from her.

Max is a kindergartener who his highly sensitive to auditory and visual input. He is happiest in a quiet room with one or two other people. He has an older sister who is very quiet and their home tends to be quiet and calm. Busy classrooms, or even after school activities, like drawing class, are overwhelming for him. He prefers to sit with his body facing away from the main classroom area and takes frequent breaks to go to the restroom. He wears his hoodie pulled up over his head to dampen the classroom noises. To others, he looks inattentive and unresponsive in a busy and noisy environment, when actually he is quite overwhelmed and is simply blocking out extra sounds and images in order to manage his behavior.

AUDITORY

Auditory input, or sound, is useful in identifying where we are in space. It helps us interpret visual information. People who have difficulty filtering out which sounds are important from those that are unimportant can find this uncertainty to be very distressing. These individuals might misinterpret auditory cues, feel overwhelmed, or have difficulty settling down. For some children, having a low volume, steady, monotonous sound playing (i.e., white noise) can mask distracting noises and thus help dampen their internal auditory system. Some children have a higher threshold for auditory input. Those children may seek out noises and generate a lot of noise themselves.

VISUAL

The visual sense, or sight, works in conjunction with our auditory and vestibular systems to help us interpret the environment. Your eyes, in combination with the vestibular system, help maintain an upright position as your body moves in order to maintain balance. The visual sense is also used for locating places and things in the environment, and obtaining more detailed information about objects. Visual processing deficits can be seen when a child has difficulty functioning successfully in a bright, highly decorated classroom or crowded shopping mall. Some children seem to have blinders on—they can't find their missing book though it was sitting on their desk all along. Reducing the amount of visual stimulation can help a child to focus on what is important and necessary for a task, or lend their attention to other sensory systems or behavior.

ORAL

The oral system can be broken down into two parts. First is our gustatory sense, or taste. The second is the oral tactile component which is our focus in this book. Babies use their mouths to explore texture, taste, and attributes of objects. As they grow, children typically continue this exploration and learning with their hands and fingers (tactile), and less with their mouths (oral). However, there are those children who continue to chew on toys, seek out strong flavors, and put non-food items in their mouths just to experience the textures. These individuals are said to have under-responsive oral tactile systems. Other children cannot tolerate various food textures in or on their mouths and may even have an overactive gag reflex. These individuals tend to have a hyper-, or over-responsive oral tactile system.

OLFACTORY

The sense of smell, olfactory sense, is special in that the information received from the environment goes directly to the part of our brain that also supports emotion, behavior, and motivation. Because of this, things that register with the olfactory system can cause a strong reaction in a child. Food preferences are guided by smell, so if a child is easily overwhelmed by smells he may not want to try different foods. Soaps and perfumes can cause avoidance behaviors, and familiar scents can be calming to an individual. Smell is an important, yet often neglected sense to keep in mind.

CHARACTERISTICS TYPICAL OF A CHILD WITH ORAL AND/OR OLFACTORY SENSITIVITY

chews clothing or personal items

enjoys strong flavors such as pickles, salsa, vinegar, sour candy

eats mostly bland foods such as chicken, french fries, potato chips, plain pasta, bread

sensitive to perfumes, shampoos, or deodorants

CHARACTERISTICS TYPICAL OF A CHILD WITH AUDITORY AND/OR VISUAL SENSITIVITY

does not respond immediately, or responds inconsistently when spoken to

appears inattentive

highly sensitive to noise

covers ears in public restrooms, classroom, or auditorium

overreacts to applause, cheers, or other loud noises

seems disinterested or disengaged in group activities

walks with head down in busy or crowded environments

freezes or withdraws upon entering a room with a lot of activity

closes eyes or covers eyes in bright lights

difficulty finding desired object in complex background such as pantry, desk, sock drawer

In this chapter

Sensory Garden
Page 92

Sound Snake
Page 96

Hiding Bag
Page 100

Super Simple Projects
Page 99, 103-104

Shelby and Noah explore a Sensory Garden.

Sensory Garden

Let's get outside! Gardening can be a wonderful sensory experience all on its own, so why not make a garden specifically for sensory exploration? This project is endlessly adaptable to your climate and space.

A sensory garden can range from a potted herb on a windowsill to a large backyard area filled with many textures, scents, and sounds. The directions below are for a garden that would fit in the corner of a backyard. When creating your sensory garden, be sure to include things your little gardener would enjoy. Will you add textured plants, sand or rocks to touch; visual features, such as a windmill or metallic streamers; or scented herbs to smell as you water your garden? As much as possible, include your child in the design, planting, and maintenance of the garden. Watering and tending the plants is all part of the sensory experience— get messy!

Consider using recycled materials like tires to hold the soil. Wooden planters or sturdy pots would work just as well for your container garden.

MATERIALS

For a recycled tire garden as shown in the photos

5 tires, four larger and one smaller, least two the same width

4 bolts (¼ inch width and 1.5 to 2 inches long) with nuts and 8 washers

Drill with 3/8 inch or larger drill bit

4 large bags of potting soil

Your choice of plants and other accessories as listed on page 95

Four 50-pound bags of sand

Old tires are offered free of charge at most tire centers, so are an affordable container for the garden.

Supplies including bolts, nuts and washers.

Drill through the sidewall of the top tire.

Stack the tires and mark the location to drill the next tire down in the stack.

1. Drill and stack the tires. Stack two equally sized, larger tires. Using a large drill bit, drill through one sidewall of a tire in two locations. Set this tire on the other, same size tire. Push a pen through the hole in the sidewall to mark the hole location on the tire underneath. Remove the top tire and drill through the sidewall of the bottom tire in the marked locations. Repeat this procedure with the smaller tire on top of the stacked tires. The smaller tire will be off to one side so the holes will be drilled in the area where the surfaces touch.

2. Attach the tires. At all four locations, put a washer on a bolt and push the bolt through both layers of tire. Slip on another washer and then the nut. Hand tighten.

3. Position the tires. Arrange the two additional tires around the tire stack and position the entire arrangement in the garden space.

4. Fill with potting soil and plants. Fill the tire stack and one of the tires on the ground with potting soil and plant the various plants. Keep in mind plants with upright habits or trailing habits and include a mix of height, color and texture in each pot. Fill the remaining tire with sand.

5. Complete the garden by adding pinwheels, glass beads or stones, wind chimes or any other embellishments your child will enjoy. Add toys to the sandbox including shovels, rakes, sifters and small objects to hide in the sand.

What to include in the garden

Tactile: Textured plants such as lamb's ears, feathered grasses, hardy succulents or wooly thyme. Other features can include stones, wood borders, glass beads, textured tires or other pots.

Olfactory: Scented plants including rosemary, oregano, mint, lavender, and flowers of all sorts.

Taste: For a perennial planting and year-round flavor, herbs are perfect. For seasonal flavors, try small fruits such as blueberries and strawberries or even dwarf fruit trees.

Auditory: Tall grasses that swish, water features, wind chimes and (if it won't disturb the neighbors) consider hanging old pots and pans in the garden for children to bang on.

Visual: Plants that move in the wind, Mylar garden ornaments, or a pinwheel. A small fountain or water feature. Choose plants or flowers with a variety of colors.

Your local Master Gardeners organization, cooperative extension, or any regional garden book can help you select plants appropriate to your climate and soil type. Also consider whether you want to garden regularly and replace annual plants seasonally, or if perennial plantings would be a better choice for your family.

Push the bolt through both tires and secure the nut.

Once tires are secure, fill with soil/sand.

Add plants!

Add other sensory elements such as glass beads, wind chimes, pin wheels and more.

CHEAPER

Divide existing plants and replant them in the sensory garden. This works especially well for mint and clumping grasses.

Use smaller containers that require less soil, or plant directly into a patch of earth.

FANCIER

Add a small recirculating fountain as a water feature.

Tai tries to identify what is making the sound inside the Sound Snake.

Sound Snake

For children who seek out auditory input wherever they can, this toy will be quite engaging. This snake helps children fulfill their need to hear and experience certain sounds but also puts limits on the sounds they can make. Each section should be filled with a variety of noisemakers that produce sounds preferred by the child so the child will seek it out. Know what types of sound your child gravitates to and start collecting ways to reproduce those noises.

This project is a step up from the Fidget Bag on page 72. The separate compartments in the snake ensure each sound can be isolated and contained. However, the connectedness of the snake provides an added twist as producing a sound in one section can often cause neighboring compartments to be triggered. Younger children especially like this toy.

MATERIALS

Two strips of lightweight, knit fabric each 4 by 22 inches

Six different noisemakers

Strong glue such as Super Glue

Machine sewing supplies

A recycled t-shirt makes perfect fabric for this project.

NOISEMAKERS

Crinkly packaging such as a chip bag

A bottle lid that pops when pressed (Snapple lids really do pop better than other, similar lids)

Jingle bell or bell cat toy

Loose beads made of glass, plastic, wood, or metal

Small metal tins or plastic containers (breath mint containers or small Easter eggs are perfect) filled with: rice, beans, sand, poly pellets. buttons, washers or pennies. Or, any of the above along with a cotton ball to dampen noise

Various noisemakers. The Snapple lids are definitely better than other, similar lids.

The "snake" is sewn and ready for the noisemakers.

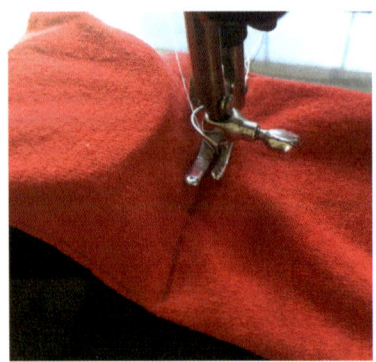

Sewing the first noisemaker into place.

1. Prepare the noisemakers. Fill the containers with small amounts of various contents and shake them to test the sound. You may also want to let your child explore the different noisemakers before you finalize them to see which are the most preferred. Once the noises are chosen and containers are filled, glue the containers closed. Allow the glue to dry.

2. Sew the snake. Place the two strips of fabric good sides together and sew down one long side, across the bottom and up the other long side leaving a narrow end open. Turn the snake right out.

3. Make the sections. Starting at the closed end, mark horizontal lines approximately every 3.5 inches using the disappearing pen or chalk.

4. Insert the noisemakers. Push the first noisemaker into the snake and sew across the first line to secure it in place. Continue adding noisemakers and stitching them in place until the snake is full. At the end of the snake, tuck in the raw edges of the fabric and stitch the opening closed. Then trim any loose threads—your snake is ready to make sounds.

CHEAPER

Using recycled materials as described above makes this project very affordable.

EASIER

Create the noisemakers minus the snake. Keep them in a box for your child to use.

FANCIER

Add a tongue when sewing the snake closed in step 4. Also sew or draw on some eyes. Consider adding texture to the body. Embellish the snake with paint or fabric markers—give it some real personality. Use the Weighty Worm on page 31 for inspiration.

PRIVACY BARRIER

During quiet reading or independent work time, try using a barrier system to prevent unwanted visual stimuli. Tape together 3 folders, or use an old cardboard shipping box cut to form a horseshoe shape, to create a privacy wall around the desktop.

CALMING BOTTLES

Fill an empty water bottle 1/2-2/3 of the way with hot water then fill with clear school glue, and if you have it, a tablespoon of glycerin. Next, choose glitter in either the super fine, standard size, or both. Add sequins if desired. Glue on the lid before use! When children need to calm themselves, they can shake the bottle and watch as the glitter settles over several minutes. This is a visual calming technique that also provides that few minutes of cool down time that many children need during a distressing situation or before resolving the problem at hand.

Jack searches for the red car in the Hiding Bag.

Hiding Bag

The hiding bag is full of treasures that can be personal-ized for each child. It is a great way to keep kids busy during quiet times like church, meetings, or assemblies or during rides in the car or bus. It is perfect for kids whose hands need to be doing something at all times and it is easy to transport! The hiding bag can also be used as game to improve visual perceptual skills, similar to a game of "I Spy."

MATERIALS

1/8 yard clear vinyl, cut into a 4.5 x 4.5-inch square

Scrap of sturdy fabric, such as home decor fabric, at least 8 x 16 inches

2-2.5 cups of poly pellets

10-15 small, unbreakable objects to hide, such as plastic animals, coins, dice, buttons, plastic magnet letters, marbles.

Vinyl comes in several weights and is often sold for table covers. Feel the various weights and choose one that is pliable and easy to manipulate but sturdy enough to not be easily pierced. A mid-weight vinyl such as 12 gauge works perfectly.

The volume of poly pellets you need will depend on how many objects you are hiding. Overfilling with pellets will make the bag harder to manipulate and the "hiding" objects harder to detect.

Choose smooth-edged items to hide; objects with sharp edges may poke holes in the bag.

The second set of 4.5 inch wide strips is being sewn to the vinyl. Note that you will trim the ends to a square after sewing.

The front is pinned to sew to the back. The back should be good side up!

Objects to hide plus pellets.

Sewing the bag closed once pellets are inside. Note that raw edges are tucked in.

1. Cut pieces for the bag. Cut vinyl to make a 4.5 inch square. Cut a 7.5 inch square out of the fabric. Then cut 2 inch wide strips from the remaining fabric. You'll need two strips that are 4.5 inches long and two that are 7.5 inches long.

2. Make fabric borders. Put the 4.5 inch long strip face down on the vinyl and sew with a ¼ inch seam. Put the other 4.5 inch strip on the opposite side of the vinyl square and sew again. If needed (and very carefully) iron fabric back away from vinyl. Take care not to touch the iron to the vinyl. Fold the fabric strips back and add the longer strips to the other sides.

3. Sew the bag. Place the vinyl square with borders face down onto the backing square so right sides are together. Pin and stitch around edges leaving about 3 inches open on one side. Clip excess fabric from the corners and turn right side out.

4. Fill the bag. Fill the bag with poly pellets and small objects making sure it is not too full which makes it hard to manipulate. Carefully pin closed the opening with raw edges tucked in. Top stitch the opening closed.

CHEAPER AND EASIER

Put the objects in a sturdy zippered plastic bag. Fill the container with rice rather than poly pellets and secure the top with duct tape. A clear vinyl pencil pouch is another pre-made container option and a plastic bottle or jar can work but be sure to leave room for the rice to move around and expose the hidden treasures.

FANCIER

Use all objects starting with the same letter--perhaps the first letter of your child's name--or use all objects in the same, favorite color

Attach a written or pictorial list of objects to search for

Choose fabric that is personalized for your child

SCENTED TOOLS

For kids who need a little extra input during the day, you can create tools that target the olfactory system (sense of smell). For calming, use a bit of lavender, vanilla, jasmine or rosemary. Add dried lavender to a favorite stuffed animal, to your laundry as it goes through the dryer, or a couple of drops of essential oil to their hand lotion. You can add a few drops of essential oil to a cotton ball and store it in an old film canister or other small plastic container, to take out and sniff when needed. For alerting, try using citrus, cinnamon, or peppermint essential oils.

Commercially available products, such as Smencils, and Mr. Sketch Markers offer scented options for writing and coloring.

AQUARIUM TUBE PENCIL TOPPER

Plastic tubing can be purchased at the hardware store for less than a dollar a foot. Buy tubing with 5/16 inch interior dimension--it should fit snugly over the eraser. Cut off a 1 ½ inch length and put it on the end of a pencil over the eraser. It gives children who need oral stimulation something appropriate to chew on during school and saves the tops of their pencils.

This is not appropriate for younger children as it is a choking hazard.

SECRET ROOM

Make a secret room by draping a sheet or blanket over a small table, desk, or other surface to block out excess light and movement. Not only will this promote attention to task, but it can help with self-calming when a child is overstimulated. Put a Target Crash Pillow (see page 34) under the table to make the space even more cozy.

auditory projects

WHITE NOISE

Babies can be quieted by a gentle "hushhhhh," or the hum of the fan. The same is true for older children. White noise can be simulated with specific machines, radios, apps, and household items (like a fan). Find a sound that your child finds soothing, like a waterfall, or city traffic. Play this sound when your child is sleeping to prevent wake-ups, or play through headphones for loud, busy events. Similar options include noise cancelling headphones and earplugs.

SOUND SHAKERS

Fill small empty containers with different items (rice, beans, small washers, plastic beads) to create a fun game that builds auditory discrimination skills. As the child shakes them, they can try to identify what is in each one. You can recycle plastic Easter eggs or small butter containers. To dampen and change the sound, add cotton balls. For a fancier version, see Sound Snake.

CONCERT WALL

Some children enjoy making noise, just to make noise. Why not give them an outlet to do so using old pots and pans, pie tins, and wooden boards. Provide a stick or dowel to use to create a beat all of their own! If you have items and space to dedicate to this purpose, create a "wall" with hooks or pegs where each noisemaker can hang. Your child can move the items around and experiment with banging them in a different order.

This book is mostly about things you can *make* to support sensory processing but there are a lot of things you can *do* to complement the tools in this book and help children with sensory challenges. We thought it would be helpful to include an activity list as a reference to use as you are discovering your child's individual needs and preferences.

As in the rest of this book, we've categorized these suggestions by sensory system but there is definitely a lot of overlap.

ACTIVITIES THAT PROVIDE PROPRIOCEPTIVE INPUT

Apply deep pressure input or joint compression through activities such as pushing and pulling a wagon or laundry basket or playing tug-o-war

Massage while applying lotion after bathtime

Jump on trampoline or pogo stick, or with a jump rope

Play "animal walks," taking large, heavy stomps like a dinosaur, walking on all fours like a cat

Crash into a Target Crash Pillow or a pile of pillows

Play squish, making the child into a hot dog or sandwich with pillows

Try swimming or martial arts

Dig in wet sand

Play on monkey bars or other playground equipment

Obstacle courses

Make games out of strengthening activities such as push ups, sit ups, or wheelbarrow walking

Practice yoga with your child

WAYS TO SUPPORT VESTIBULAR PROCESSING

Make sure to offer movement seekers:

A wiggle cushion on the chair

Active movement breaks

Slow, rhythmic movement (like swinging back and forth) for calming

Fast, multi-directional movement (like spinning, trampoline) for alerting

Activities that promote postural control, static strength and endurance

Tips for movement avoiders:

Start by helping the child move in directions that they are best able to tolerate. Once you have their confidence, you can vary the input slightly as tolerated.

Never force a child to engage in a movement activity; this will trigger a "fight or flight" response and negative behaviors.

Allow the child to have time to explore new environments or equipment that may be distressing.

Use distraction techniques to take their mind off of a possible scary and challenging activity.

Try linear movement before rotary, as it is easier to tolerate.

Provide proprioceptive input prior to or during movement activities, to improve their tolerance for movement.

WAYS TO SUPPORT TACTILE PROCESSING

Apply deep pressure—such as bear hugs, squishes, firm pressure on back or shoulders, arms and legs—prior to grooming activities, hair-cutting, or dental visits

Use firm touch with baths, hair-washing, hair combing, grooming

Use "training toothpaste" because it is less foamy

Buy clothing made of cotton and flannel instead of polyester

Buy used clothing or use hand-me-downs that are already broken in

Choose clothes without tags

Try spandex clothing, which provides a firmer touch to the body

Use sunscreen sticks for those who cannot tolerate lotions

Have your child be a line leader or caboose to prevent unexpected touch while waiting in line

Have your child sit at the end of a table instead of between children to allow for a bigger "space bubble"

Allow child to direct their participation with tactile activities

Offer tactile fidgets at school or during waiting times

SUGGESTIONS FOR THE OTHER SENSES

Wear a hoodie to block out peripheral visual information

Face desk to a blank wall in the classroom or sit in front of the class to reduce visual distractions

Have only one or two things on desk/table at at time

Use a slant board such as a closed three ring binder to help visual focus with written work and reading

Learn different strategies for scanning, tracking, and reading to improve speed and efficiency

Use perfume-free soaps, detergents, and cleaners

Apply peppermint oil on pads under the nose to improve alertness

Wear sunglasses outdoors or in indoor bright environments

Use noise dampening headphones

Prepare child ahead of time when attending events where there will be applause or cheering

Allow child to chew gum if appropriate for age; incorporate crunchy, chewy foods during the day to satisfy the need to chew or bite

Noah reading on a One-Legged Stool

Resources and further reading

BOOKS FOR PROFESSIONALS

Ayres, Ph.D., J.A. **Sensory Integration and the Child: Understanding Hidden Sensory Challenges**. Revised and Updated by Pediatric Therapy Network. Los Angeles, CA: Western Psychological Services. 2005.

Bundy, A.C., S.J. Lane, and E.A. Burray. **Sensory Integration Theory and Practice**, 2nd ed. Philadelphia: F.A. Davis Company, 1991.

Corson, OTR/L, D. and Green, OTD R/L, A. **A Guide to Implementing Sensory Strategies in the Classroom Setting**. Stuart, FL: Solutions For Therapists, 2009.

BOOKS FOR PARENTS

Biel, M.A., OTR/L, L. and Peske, N. **Raising a Sensory Smart Child: The Definitive Handbook for Helping Your Child with Sensory Processing Issues**. New York, NY: The Penguin Group. 2005. http://www.sensorysmarts.com/index.html

Kranowitz, M.A., C. **The Out-of-Sync Child: Recognizing and Coping with Sensory Processing Disorder.** (Revised and Updated). New York, NY: The Penguin Group, 2005. http://out-of-sync-child.com/

Kranowitz, M.A., C. **The Out-of-Sync Child has Fun: Activities for Kids with Sensory Integration Dysfunction**. New York, NY: The Penguin Group, 2003.

Abraham, D., Heffron, C., Braley, P., and Drobnjak, L. **Sensory Processing 101**. Sensory Processing 101, 2015. http://sensoryprocessing101.com/

WEBSITES

Sensory Processing Disorder Foundation - Research and education. http://www.spd-foundation.net/

Sensory Processing Disorder (SPD) - General information, activity ideas, resources. http://www.sensory-processing-disorder.com/

Project Sensory - Information, resources and tools. http://www.projectsensory.com/

Lemon Lime Adventures - Blog with a focus on sensory processing, activity ideas, and information. http://lemonlimeadventures.com

Acknowledgements

This book would not have been possible without friends and family who gave their time and expertise. Thank you!

Photography:
KARIN HIGGINS STURGIS

Graphic design consultation:
LISA WELLS

Editing:
SUSAN HERMAN
edit2yourcredit.com

Art for system icons:
TAI HACKETT

Chalkboard art for cover
PAIGE HAWORTH

Thank you to the families who provided their adorable children as models. And to our models who put up with all sorts of directions and made each project shine.

PAIGE	**EMERY**
CHARLIE	**JAY**
KYSON	**HEATHER**
DECLAN	**TAI**
MCKENNA	**RUSSELL**
CASEY	**ROXY**
ERIK	**EMMA**
SHELBY	**CARLOS**
COLBY	**EVIE**
ANNA	**JACK**
JACOB	**CAMILLA**
NOAH	

Acknowledgements

Thank you SO MUCH to everyone who supported us on Kickstarter!

Allison Chilcott

Andrew Fishman

Ash Harper

Beth and Mark Duede

Blythe and Hannah Ardyson

Brian E. Micek

Carole and John Schuch

Courtney Kaull

Deana Lewis

Elisabeth Schramm

Emily McDougall

Gayle Dax-Conroy

Jamie Hubbard

Jamie Law

Jane Robertson

Jessie Poteat

Jodi W.

Kate Burwinkel

Kathy Kelly

Kelly M Caponera

Krista Shultz & Cari Ingrassia

Kyle Rogers

Laura Muro

Laura Slaughter

Lindsey and Gabe

Lisa Wells

Mark Beckwith

Martha Ozonoff

Megan

Melissa Neff

Melissa Reese

Michelle

Michelle Lippert

Miracle Girl

Mitchel Benson

Narelle

Parker Broaddus

Robert LeSueur

Sam T.

Savuth

Shelly Williams

Susan Farias

Susan Huffman

Swistle

The Nest: A Gathering Place

Toria

Yvonne

About the Authors

Kristin Cockrell, MOT, OTR/L, is a pediatric occupational therapist with 15 years of experience working with children in both clinical and school settings. In addition to raising three children--one who has sensory processing disorder--she is an owner and director at Color, Construct, Create Studios, a therapeutic art program for children based in San Diego, California.

Find Kristin online at www.colorconstructcreate.com.

Melissa Haworth started sewing weighted blankets for a friend's therapy practice and realized that there wasn't a comprehensive book of instructions to make tools and toys to support sensory processing. She has taught a variety of sewing classes around Sacramento, California and in addition to maintaining a personal crafting blog she has contributed to books and magazines.

Find Melissa online at underconstructionblog.typepad.com

Check out: DIYsupertoys.com

Printed in Great Britain
by Amazon